Harry James-Trumpet Icon

The Music of the 20th Century's Trumpet Player

By Chuck Par-Due

Harry James-Trumpet Icon

Table of Contents

This book is dedicated to our Friends

Viola Monte who has been the glue that kept it all together

Dick Maher (1930-2017) designated by Harry James as the official Band historian.

I could always trust Dick to cut through untruths and legends.

Find us on Facebook @ Harry James Music Appreciation Group

Forward

What a pleasure! Finally, a highly regarded musician has written a book about my Dad (Harry James) and his actual musical skills and playing experiences!

Both Chuck Par-Due and his extremely talented singer wife Cheryl Morris (Par-Due) are excellent musicians and have both actually been part of my Dad's musical Family. As far as I am concerned, that alone makes both of them highly qualified to write a book about him. If both of them weren't far above average in their musical skills, Dad would never have been associated with them!

Dad had a photographic memory in addition to his unusual incredible musical talents. What most musicians worked so hard to accomplish Dad usually accomplished in a single setting. He also had a gift for mathematics – and music is based on mathematics. These items together allowed him to become a unique and gifted musical virtuoso.

This book finally delves into my Dad's actual musical skills and his interactions with his contemporaries. It is based upon various conversations that skilled musicians have amongst themselves. What a wonderful concept (for a change)!

Thank you, Chuck and Cheryl! I'll finally have a book about my Father that I can treasure for its actual facts! I suspect that hundreds of thousands of gifted musicians around the world – and many fine musical institutions - will also treasure this great book.

Harry James Jr.

Preface

In the final scenes of the 2019 Superhero film "Avengers-Endgame," Captain America (Steve Rogers) retires to the past to finally have that dance with Peggy and marry the love of his life.

The musical soundtrack used to show the emotional impact of that scene was the 1945 recording of "It's Been a Long, Long, Time" by Harry James, with vocalist Kitty Kallen. This was the second Avengers movie in which the James recording was featured.

There is little doubt that no single musical recording, evokes the sentimentality of the end of World War II, and the emotional reunions, and losses, of that event, like this Harry James recording.

Harry James was second only perhaps to Glenn Miller, as a successful Band Leader.

Adding that success to James' triumphs as a Movie and TV star, and the fact that no single Jazz trumpet player from that era, combined power, technical skills, and incredible improvisational ability, separates Harry James from all other trumpet players from the Big Band Era.

Harry James began to engender notoriety among Jazz musicians while he was still in his teens.

The purpose of this book is to delve into Harry James, the Musician. It isn't fair to anyone to dissect his personal life at this point.

I make no apologies for believing that Harry James was the greatest trumpet player of all time, in the eyes of millions of people all over the World, including Me. and his musical legacy needs to be shared.

Chuck Par-Due

A Very Special Thanks...

A very special heartfelt thanks to all of the following, for the parts you have played in my development as a Musician...

My Dad, Jesse Pearl, William Bobrick, Viola Monte, Frank Monte, Harry James, who have left us.

To my Daughter Virginia Par-Due Braucher for her artistic talents, and design of the front cover of this book.

Peggy Essex-Klammer, Carlos Guzman, Clay Fisher, Denny Ilett, and Derek Saidak.

To my Friend Chris LaBarbera, who's been my sounding board.

A King-sized thank you to my Friend Chris Charvat at the H.N. White Company.

I especially wish to thank all of you who had a part in the development of this book...

My wife Cheryl, the late Dick Maher, Mike Butera, Chris Charvat, Tony Crapis, Bill Barrett, Les DeMerle, Hal Espinosa, Marty Harrell, Alan Kaplan, Tommy Porrello, Tony Scodwell, and Dave Stone.

Also, Fred Radke, Michael Millar, Jim Maher, and Bill Hicks.

Thanks also to Hallei Montalbano.

A special thanks to our Friend Harry James Jr.

Most of all, thanks to the members of the "Harry James Music Appreciation Group" on Facebook for your support.

The Formative Years

The stories about the childhood of Harry Haag James have been well documented.

Born to Circus parents, Harry James did not get to experience a "normal" childhood.

To Everette and Maybelle James, the Circus Life was the life they chose. Travel, hardship, and instability were faced daily.

Maybelle James was a famed trapeze artist and an operatic prima-donna. The expectant Mrs. James continued to work on the high wire until shortly before the birth of her son.

The young boy Harry acquired several skills from the adults who were employed with the Circus. The foremost ability being how to be a contortionist.

Though not a desirable skill set in today's world, it was a staple skill in the Three-ring Circus.

Harry was billed as "The World's Youngest Contortionist" with The Mighty Haag Circus. The stories were told that even as a small boy, Harry was quite talented. However, a mastoid condition forced the demise of his budding career as a contortionist.

At the same time, Harry began to show an interest in his Father's career...music.

Everette James was quite well known as a first-rate musical conductor and cornet soloist. He possessed a classically trained technique on the cornet. Also, he was a gifted high note player.

Harry regaled in telling the stories of his Dad's daring to play in the altissimo range of the cornet, long before the term "screeching" had ever been applied to a brass instrument.

At the age of four, Harry began to learn to play the drums. He took to the new skill instantly. By the age of six, he was playing a full trap set with the Circus band.

Around the age of eight, a trumpet player in the Circus band began to teach the boy how to play the cornet. By the time Everette James found out about it, Harry had attained a level of proficiency that left any doubt as to where Harry's career was headed.

Initially, Harry's father was dead set against Harry becoming a musician. But it wasn't long before the elder James succumbed to the inevitable and began to teach the nine-year-old Harry James proper technique.

Everette James planned for Harry to travel a "legit" classical path on the cornet.

The elder James was quite demanding in his requirements for his young son and his practice regimen. Everette would select several pages of Etudes from the Arban book for Harry to perfect.

Harry, being a quick study, longed to join his friends on the baseball field. Harry was also a gifted athlete and was sought after as a teen by at least two Major League baseball teams.

The rules were quite clear. When Harry could play his assigned trumpet exercises, then he was free to play baseball.

However, Everette James required perfect execution of the assigned exercises. If Harry missed even one note, he had to start from the beginning, until he could play it perfectly.

By the age of eleven, Harry was leading the full Circus band, and playing his Father's trumpet parts.

He became known among the Circus musicians who crossed his path while he was only thirteen years old. His father, Everette James, was well known among the cornetists of the day. Both as a Band Leader, and a cornet player and teacher.

The teenaged Harry James was whispered about as a lead trumpet player and soloist of incredible skills and power. By the age of fifteen, Harry James was playing lead and solo trumpet in regional bands.

At the age of seventeen, he was approached by Band Leader Ben Pollack, who led a Dixieland-tinged band. Pollack was instrumental in the careers of Benny Goodman, Jack Teagarden, Charlie Spivak, Glenn Miller, and many others.

Harry James joined Ben Pollack in 1936. His mates in the trumpet section were Charlie Spivak and Shorty Sherock. Spivak was the designated lead trumpet player, but it soon became apparent that the young Harry James was a superior leader of any trumpet section he joined.

Spivak soon left and joined the fledgling Glenn Miller band.

Ben Pollack immediately began to give James featured numbers. It was apparent to record buyers, that Harry James played trumpet differently than any other trumpeter.

Harry James' style of playing Jazz, was a combination of the majestic, soaring style of Louis Armstrong and the ripping style of Muggsy Spanier. Harry also was fascinated by Bix Beiderbecke's harmonic sense. Beiderbecke started on the piano. And much like Charlie Shavers, a few years later, the chordal sense in Bix Beiderbecke's improvisations was superior to the average trumpet player of his day.

In a 1938 Down Beat interview, Harry listed Armstrong and Spanier as his favorite trumpet players. He also mentioned he enjoyed listening to Berigan and Bix a great deal.

Added to Harry's Jazz delivery, was a lyrical approach matched only by Johnny Hodges and Ben Webster on saxophones.

The Goodmans

By late 1935, Benny Goodman had ascended to the top of the ever-growing Swing music industry. From a personality standpoint, Benny Goodman was ill-prepared to be the "King of Swing." He was self-absorbed and possessed no communication or people skills. The "Goodman Ray" was an authentic fact among members of his bands over the years.

Two of Benny Goodman's brothers were members of this band in 1936. Harry was a bass player, and Irving Goodman played in the trumpet section. Irving had experience working with difficult, and even temperamental band leaders, having played with Bunny Berigan, the always feuding Dorsey Brothers, Alvino Ray, and Charlie Barnet, among others.

Being Benny Goodman's brother in Benny's band, could not have been an enviable position.

In retrospect, we will never know how long Irving Goodman had looked for a polite way out of his brother's band. However, when Irving heard a recording by the Ben Pollack Band called "Deep Elm," he knew he had found an out.

In December of 1936, Irving Goodman approached his brother Benny to tell him he wanted out of the band. Before Benny could put up an argument, Irving told Benny not to worry, because he found a replacement, and the replacement would be an upgrade over Irving's playing.

The replacement would be Harry James, a twenty-year-old player in Ben Pollack's band.

Irving tracked Harry down by phone. James was in Los Angeles; Benny and the band were in New York City. Irving told Harry that Benny wanted him to join the Goodman band.

Harry agreed.

Excitedly, Irving announced to Benny that he had hired Harry. Benny's response was, "Can he get here tomorrow?"

Irving told him it would take several days to get from Los Angeles by train.

The next day, Benny Goodman officially hired Harry James for $150 a week by telegram.

The story of Harry's first night with Benny Goodman is legendary.

Benny had a Benny Goodman Trio gig; at the same time, the band was playing at the Congress Hotel. Lionel Hampton was leading the group from the drum seat.

Lionel called up a stock arrangement of "A Fine Romance" and offered a chorus to the new trumpet player. Harry played such an exciting solo that Hampton told him to play another and another. Harry James played five choruses during a dinner set.

The entire Goodman Band took notice.

Not only did Harry James, Ziggy Elman, and Chris Griffin make an incredible trumpet section, but the three became fast friends.

All three trumpet men were first-class lead players and sight-readers.

From Ziggy Elman, Harry learned how to use Jewish or "Froelich" style phrasing, which became a permanent part of Harry's playing.

Chris Griffin was a great lead player and a well-disciplined musician. Harry learned a great deal about blending in a section from Griffin.

Harry James immediately inherited most of the solos that had been recorded by Bunny Berigan. He added intensity and drive to the Goodman Band that it never had.

Bunny Berigan was the soloist on the Goodman record of "King Porter Stomp," however, the solo by Harry James from a 1938 air shot, has been the pattern for most arrangements since, including Doc Severinsen and the Tonight Show band.

Soon not only other musicians but the record-buying public began to recognize the tall, skinny trumpet player from Texas.

A perfect example of Harry's influence on the Goodman Band can be heard on a radio broadcast from 1938.

During the performance of the St. Louis Blues, at 2:54 of the tune, the audience erupts in applause at merely seeing Harry James rising from the trumpet section.

The resultant solo by James did not disappoint. And then at the end of Harry's solo, James took over the lead from Ziggy Elman driving toward the climax of the Blues.

After only one year with the Goodman Band, Harry recorded a set of sides with his own studio band. The band was a combination of sidemen from Count Basie and Goodman bands.

Harry's playing on these records convey a musical maturity beyond his 22 years of age. His playing was self-assured and even aggressive. The musicians who backed Harry on the session immediately recognized Harry James as one of them.

Everyone knew that there was no doubt that Harry James would soon have his own band.

It was with the Benny Goodman Orchestra that Harry James first met Frank Montalbano (ne Monte). He was nicknamed "Pee Wee" because of his diminutive stature. Monte was the "Band Boy" for Benny, having come from the Hal Kemp Orchestra.

Frank Monte and Harry James formed a Friendship and partnership that lasted until James died in 1983.

Harry's Equipment

Much discussion has occurred over the last eighty years about Harry James' choices of trumpets and mouthpieces.

When Harry James began to play the trumpet at the age of ten years old, the instrument his father Everette gave him to learn on was a King Master cornet.

Many famed cornetists of the day played the King Master cornets. Some of them who at one time played King were Merle Evans, Herbert L. Clarke, King Oliver, and Del Staigers were among those who blew a King Master cornet.

By the time Harry had begun playing in bands at the age of fifteen, he was playing a King Liberty trumpet.

Around the same time, Harry began using a Heim 2 mouthpiece. Gustav Heim was a renowned German trumpet player, who when he came to America in 1904, became principal trumpeter with the Boston and New York Philharmonic, among others.

Heim was famous for playing a very deep trumpet mouthpiece, which gave him an almost Teutonic sound on his trumpet.

Frank Holton, the founder of the Holton Musical Instrument Company, began to make two Heim mouthpieces. The Heim 1 was a more conventional commercial mouthpiece, while Heim 2 was a deep mouthpiece producing a deep tone. It was not easy to play.

Interestingly, Heim 2 was the preferred mouthpiece of Miles Davis.

It may have been recommended to the young Harry James by another trumpet player, or perhaps even his Dad Everette.

Nonetheless, Harry James played the Heim 2 when he began his professional career, a testament to the strength of Harry's chops even then.

Shortly after joining Benny Goodman, Harry decided to start playing a Selmer Trumpet. Partly from the influence of his section mates Griffin and Elman, who both played Selmer, and because

Harry's idol Louis Armstrong was already Selmer's foremost endorsee.

It is unclear whether Selmer gave Harry the set of two trumpets in 1937, or whether Harry paid for them himself.

The story often told is that Harry had set the trumpet case on the ground behind the band bus. He got on the bus forgetting that his prize trophies were still behind the bus. The driver put the bus in reverse and flattened Harry's toys.

He still had his old trumpet, so he played that one until Selmer could get him two more.

Sometime in the Spring of 1938, the Benny Goodman Orchestra was playing in New York City.

Ziggy Elman took Harry to John Parduba's shop at 140 W 49th St. Parduba had started making musical instruments in 1908. It is thought that he began making trumpet mouthpieces in 1915. He received a patent on a double-cup mouthpiece in 1935.

Ziggy had started playing the revolutionary new mouthpiece design, and convinced Harry James to try it.

After listening to Harry express his needs, Parduba began working on a custom mouthpiece just for Harry James. Once he found a design that pleased Harry, he made several more for Harry.

Parduba began to sell a "Harry James 5*" mouthpiece model, and it put the Parduba Mouthpiece Company on the map. The remarkable thing was that Harry James never played the "Harry James 5*" model. It was considerably different from Harry's custom model.

John Sr continued to make custom mouthpieces for Harry until he died in 1946

Therein was a problem.

When John Parduba Sr. died, the secret of the specifications of the mouthpieces that he made for Harry James, went to his grave with him. There were no dies or diagrams.

When John Jr. started making them for Harry, they weren't the same. John Jr. was guessing.

John Jr. tried nobly over the years to explain the dilemma to Harry James. In fact, John sent Harry a letter on May 1, 1975, in which he attempted to explain to Harry about the struggles that he was having in servicing the mouthpiece needs of his most famous customer.

"Now Harry, you say I should find one of the really old reamers to use for your cup and rim, but I must tell you that there was never a form cutting reamer for your rim and cup. The only thing I must go by are plaster impressions of your rim and cup and can only make a copy as close as possible. Some Impressions were made 35 years ago, and the last impressions I took of your mouthpiece were May 29, 1949, 25 years ago. My Dad died back in 1946, and he made your first mouthpiece practically by hand, and then impressions were taken, and from these, you can only make a copy as close as possible.

I doubt if you ever got an exact copy of the first mouthpiece you had made when you ordered a duplicate. You see, Harry, when we can't get together or be here when a mouthpiece is being made, it is very hard to solve a problem, which may be only a slight adjustment. There is no tool maker that can make a cutting form tool of your rim and cup, which would be able to make an exact copy of your mouthpiece. When the cutting tool is finished, it is so far out of the way it is ridiculous. However, I do my best under the circumstances. Sincerely yours, John Parduba."

So, combining the issues of duplication, with the changes in Harry's dental problems, and age, Harry James played the same mouthpieces made for him by Parduba in the 1940s, until the end of his life.

About trumpets, when Harry began playing Selmer brand trumpets, there was an evolution of the various models he played.

At first, Harry played the Selmer Signet model. That is the model pictured in the famous "Harry James Trumpet Method" (which Harry didn't write!)

He then played a 22B Balanced Model. Harry has often been quoted as preferring a "Balanced Model" due to the length of his long arms. It probably had more to do with the fact that Louis Armstrong played a "Balanced Model," so that's what Harry wanted.

I have played the "Balanced Model" trumpets since 1972. I don't have long arms, but that configuration is more comfortable for me.

Soon Selmer made a 25A "Harry James model" trumpet, which was gold-plated and had a .472 large bore.

Although it has been written that Harry may have played several other Selmer models over the years, these are the official records.

The story of the James-Selmer divorce was this. Supposedly Harry had asked Selmer to make a 'Harry James model' trumpet lamp. Selmer felt insulted.

Enter KING!

In 1952, Mrs. Edna White, who was now the decision-maker for the H.N. White Company, began to yield more responsibilities to her Daughter Cathryn (Kay).

"During these years, Cathryn was working hard to get big-name artists to endorse King at every opportunity. In 1952 Cathryn took

a cross country trip to call on dealers and work at a music convention in Las Vegas. Cathryn's (Kay) hard work paid off when she convinced Harry James to stop by the plant and try the new Super 20 trumpet. Harry wanted an instrument that had the valves moved forward a few inches to accommodate his long arms, and while he was in Cleveland, Mrs. White put a team of designers and craftsmen to work on his requirements. By the time that Harry left the plant, he had traded in his Selmer trumpet for an H. N. White "Super 20 Silver Sonic" and signed a deal to endorse King trumpets. Harry's first few Super '20s were normal production trumpets, but by the end of 1953, Harry took delivery of his "balanced" model. This change in trumpets and endorsement deal was due in large part because of the friendship Harry had started with Mrs. H. N. White and Cathryn. For the next thirteen years, when Harry was in Cleveland, he would stop by the King plant (to pick up a new trumpet) and would spend hours talking with "Mom White" (Edna) and would go out for an early dinner with her before going to his gig. If Harry were ever in town around the holidays, he would have dinner at Edna's house, since Harry had started with Mrs. H. N. White and Cathryn. For the next thirteen years, when Harry was in Cleveland, he would stop by the King plant (to pick up a new trumpet) and would spend hours talking with "Mom White" (Edna) and would go out for an early dinner with her before going to his gig. If Harry were ever in town around the holidays, he would have dinner at Edna's house."
(from the H.N. White Company website)

The" KING Harry James model" was a balanced model trumpet, based on the Super 20/Symphony/Silversonic model. It was a dual-bore 458/468 trumpet, with a Sterling Silver bell.

The Harry James model trumpet was never available for sale to the public. However, King would make a few horns at a time, and send them to Harry to try. The trumpets he didn't find satisfactory, would be sold by King as having been played by Harry himself. (over the years I owned two of these beautiful horns).

When the King Musical Instrument Company was sold in 1965, there were still enough parts left to build a few more horns for Harry. In 1972 King acquired Benge. From that point on, the Harry James model trumpets were differently made as from the White Company.

Former James sideman Tony Scodwell, who is a marvelous trumpet player in his own right, summed it up this way.

"I spent a fair amount of time on Harry's band in the sixties, and he was playing the King by then. Sterling silver bell with gold plated valve bodies, and [sometimes] sterling lead pipes. The bells were gold plated inside, and quite a beautiful sight they were. Dual bore and no third valve tuning slide ring. No first valve slide harp either. They were BRIGHT! Quite free blowing as well. Harry told me that he had asked a small favor of Selmer in the early fifties, and they were somewhat rude to him. Pissed him off enough to hook up with King, which he stayed with until his death. Near the end of his life, Kings were being made for him by Zig Kanstul and were very light overall. Gold plated over brass. The real gems to own are the sterling bell Kings, early to mid-60's vintage, with Harry James engraved on the side of the bell. I've made a couple of "Balanced H.J." models using a Selmer valve section from a large-bore K Modified and one with Allied valves. Both were silver-plated for no good reason. And I did have Getzen make up a balanced LB for Harry, without any tuning rings so that it would feel like the King in his hands. He didn't spend a lot of time with it before giving it back to me. I think he was interested in seeing what Doc was up to more than anything else. The question of where the length came from to "balance" the horn was answered correctly by Lawler, with the tail section of the Selmers being a fair amount longer than the tail section of the

King bells. Shorter tuning slide was the result there, and they both blow with a different feel than the "normal" configuration trumpets that we see today. Satch was the reason Harry was hooked on the Selmer early on, by the way. Tony Scodwell".

The last time I saw Harry James was three weeks before his death.

He was playing a KING gold plated trumpet with his name on it.

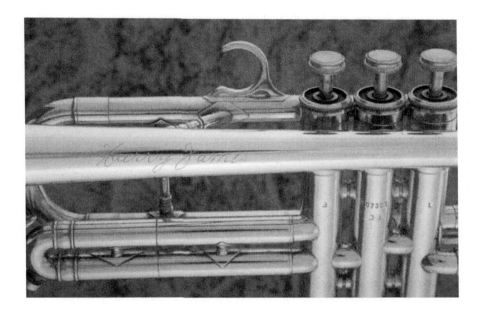

At the end of the lead pipe, was a faded old Parduba mouthpiece.

When discussing Harry's "tools" on the bandstand, he always had a jar of Vaseline on the piano, where he placed his horn and mutes. To this day, I don't fully understand why he used Vaseline the way that he did.

He rubbed it on his lips, and also on the inside of his nostrils. I am sure he had his reasons.

He also used more valve oil than any trumpet player I have ever seen. King Musical Instruments would ship him cases of King valve oil.

Although he did oil his valves in the traditional way, he also would pull the first valve slide and squeezed a lot of oil into the trumpet that way. He also would squirt it into the holes at the bottom of the valve caps.

Lastly, Harry kept a handkerchief or some other kind of rag next to his trumpet. He would rub his lips between tunes, then reapply the Vaseline.

Preparing for stardom

Within a few months of joining the Benny Goodman band, Harry's value as a sideman was being noticed by other leaders, especially on recording sessions.

Both Teddy Wilson, Red Norvo, and Lionel Hampton availed themselves of Harry's skills.

Teddy Wilson was contracted to form a recording band to back Billie Holiday on some landmark Columbia Records.

In her autography "Lady Sings the Blues," Billie Holiday told about the first time she saw Harry James. She saw James as a cocky, racist punk from Texas. (Anyone who knew Harry James, knew he was not a racist)

She tells that it required Buck Clayton to put the young trumpet virtuoso in his place. Of course, Holiday was having an affair with Buck Clayton so that she may have been biased.

The fact is that Harry James was never intimated by any trumpet player.

In January 1938, Gene Krupa left the Benny Goodman Orchestra. Krupa's outgoing personality often conflicted with the sullen, introverted Goodman. Krupa told others that he was tired of Benny "hogging" all the attention.

Many people began to ask themselves about how long before the Goodman Band's number two star, Harry James, would stay with Benny.

In January of 1938, and again in April, Harry James led an "all-star" band in the recording studio.

Again, made up of Basie and Goodman band members, they were joined on the sessions by Basie vocalist Helen Humes. Duke Ellington baritone sax star Harry Carney was also on hand.

In the January session, Herschel Evans played tenor sax.

Harry always let it be known that Herschel Evans was Harry's favorite tenor sax soloist. Their paths crossed as both were from Texas.

When Evans died of heart disease in February 1939, James began the search for tenor players that sounded close to Herschel Evans' sound. It would have been interesting to see if Evans had lived if he would have joined the new Harry James Orchestra.

The famous Carnegie Hall Concert by the Benny Goodman band on January 16.1938, did much to elevate Gene Krupa into the public sphere even more. By the end of January, Krupa was gone.

There was a brief period of about six weeks when Benny Goodman shopped for a new drummer to replace Gene Krupa. In the interim, Lionel Hampton played drums with the big band.

But who would play drums for the Benny Goodman Quartet, when Hampton manned the vibes?

Harry James!

Not enough has been said about Harry James, the drummer. He began to play drums while still wearing a toddler's diaper.

James took particular pleasure over his career, in giving the drummer with the Harry James Orchestra a break. Then Harry would sit behind the drum kit.

Later in the 1950s, when Buddy Rich would get up for a vocal, Harry would take his place.

I witnessed Harry James as a drummer several times. He was more than a competent timekeeper.

Just a Mood

Teddy Wilson was one of the greatest Jazz pianists to come out of the Swing Era. He was also a principal contractor of musicians for session work. Under the Wilson name, many of the giants of Jazz appeared on record as part of Teddy Wilson's bands.

Likewise, Red Norvo, while leading his own bands, organized "all-star" groups for record sessions.

Harry James had turned down an offer to join Red Norvo's band in 1936. Anyone who heard the young Harry James knew he was destined for stardom.

On August 29, 1937, the Benny Goodman Orchestra, and Red Norvo's band found themselves in New York.

Jazz entrepreneur John Hammond wanted to take advantage of the proximity of so many world-class musicians. He called Teddy Wilson and asked him to bring Harry James with him to a studio in New York City. He called Norvo, who resisted, but eventually obliged.

Teddy Wilson and Harry James arrived to find John Hammond, along with a bass player John Simmons. (Simmons went on to become a much sought-after bass player during the 1940s)

There was no music provided. No songs had been selected.

John Hammond simply told the four musicians, "I want to hear some blues."

There are different stories as to how the choice that they play in the key of C Sharp. (E Flat for a trumpet). For sure, Harry James didn't care what the key was. Harry loved to play ballads and blues in keys that were not popular with brass players.

There are several recordings of Harry playing popular ballads in the key of D.

Harry begins the tune with four choruses. The lyrical approach that he used in his opening firmly established Harry James as one of the best Blues players in Jazz history.

The fact was that at that time, in 1937, no other trumpet player played the way Harry James did. He was a combination of all the trumpet players he had heard growing up in East Texas.

At the age of twenty-one years old, Harry James already stood head and shoulders above the players of that time, combined with a consistency that carried him for nearly a half-century.

The Departure

In 1938, the Big Bands were now at the forefront of the American musical consciousness. Thanks to Benny Goodman, Tommy Dorsey, Artie Shaw, and others, the instrumental soloists were becoming more and more prominent.

Regarding the trumpet, Louis Armstrong was the only trumpet player who indeed was a household name. Although great players like Roy Eldridge, Buck Clayton, and several others were well known among fellow musicians and Jazz aficionados, they were nowhere close to enjoying the fame of Satchmo.

As great a player as Bunny Berigan was his instability due to his personal demons, precluded him from ever being as great a "star" among the record-buying public.

With Krupa departing from the relative safety of the Benny Goodman Orchestra, Harry James began to plot his journey into stardom.

Although Harry James was like so many successful musicians, he has some insecurities that resulted from his virtual lack of a childhood.

However, there were no insecurities when Harry James picked up a trumpet. He knew what he was capable of musically. He also was driven to capitalize on his sizable skills.

Harry became more active in Jam Sessions. Not only did this increase his visibility as a musician but helped to build his credibility among fellow musicians.

Harry's approach to jazz was an aggressive, driving, and biting attack. Combined with a knowledge of chord structures, and a fantastic ability to sight-read, Harry James used his mastery of trumpet technique to stand head and shoulders above his peers truly.

Harry James had a dream of success and a plan of where he wanted to take his music.

All he needed was money.

When Gene Krupa left Goodman's employ, Benny began to lay a groundwork for capitalizing on the eventual departure of Harry James.

In March of 1938, Goodman convinced Harry to sign with the MCA booking agency. That way, Harry could gain more opportunities as a leader. Benny Goodman hedged his bet on James' assumed success by asking a 5% commission from MCA derived from Harry's bookings.

"Ciribiribin" was an Italian Romantic waltz written by Alberto Pestalozzi in 1898.

Because of the "five notes" figure in its melody, it became a favorite for use in music instructional books for all instruments. It is probable that the young Harry James had come across it as a trumpet student.

It has been written that Harry was introduced to the song by Goodman saxophonist George Koenig.

However, on December 13, 1938, the Goodman Band recorded a new arrangement of Ciribiribin written by Fletcher Henderson. Ironically, the short trumpet solo was played by Ziggy Elman.

In September of 1938, Harry wrote his own arrangement of Ciribiribin as a feature for his extensive trumpet playing skills.

There are two Camel Caravan broadcasts where Harry played his Ciribiribin with the Goodman Band.

The James arrangement showcased all the aspects of Harry's trumpet style. It was an instant crowd-pleaser and a fitting tune for a Big Band theme song.

In December of 1938, Harry asked Benny Goodman to let him out of his contact with Goodman's band.

Goodman refused. He told Harry that he was too valuable to Benny's band. There was some truth in that. With Gene Krupa gone, Harry James was the band's biggest star.

Harry was paid $250 a week but was doubtless making much more money for Benny Goodman.

On January 11-12, 1939, Harry was called to play on a Metronome All-Star recording session.

The other trumpet players were Bunny Berigan and Sonny Dunham. Harry was the trumpet soloist on "The Blues," of which there were two takes. Harry did not play on the second side, which was "Blue Lou." Berigan and Dunham soloed on that side.

(It is somewhat ironic that Harry, being a highly functioning alcoholic later in his life, often shared the stories of seeing Bunny Berigan pulling out a flask from his hip pocket during the Metronome recording sessions)

The comparisons between Harry James and his contemporaries were inevitable.

In the mind of America's record-buying public believed that Harry James was head and shoulders above all comers.

It was time for Harry to test the waters of Independence!

Various versions of the Goodman/James parting have surfaced over the years.

Harry's version of the parting was this.

"He gave me $1900 to help me keep myself going, you know. We paid him back $20,000. Six months later, the band had hit. And Willard Alexander told Benny, "I told you not to take that deal!" "Benny had 33% of the band".

Several members told others that when Harry left the Goodman Band, the band was never the same.

So, you want to lead a band?

With approximately $2300 to work with, Harry James had an uphill climb in forming his new band.

Perhaps the biggest question that Harry faced was, determining the style that would attract the money of the public. Harry was smitten with the music of the Black bands. He was an ardent admirer of Duke Ellington and his Orchestra. For the forty-four years that Harry led his band, there was always plenty of Ellingtonia in the music. (In fact, Harry hired the Ellington band to perform at his third wedding!)

James was also a huge fan of the Jimmie Lunceford Orchestra. Many tunes in the James book were played with a decidedly Lunceford-Bounce.

However, Harry James was always a follower of Count Basie. Beginning with Harry's first recordings under his own name in 1937, musicians from Basie's band were in the sessions.

So, in January of 1939, we have a classically trained "white" trumpet player from Texas who wants to lead a "black-sounding" white band. Added to that rare combination, an emotional lyricism passed on to him by his Mother Maybelle.

Harry James was well known and liked among Texas Jazz musicians. When he began to seek out musicians for his new band, he relied heavily on his Texas connections.

The friendship between Harry James and saxophonist Dave Matthews went at least as far back as 1935. Dave Matthews had migrated from Chagrin Falls, Ohio, to Oklahoma, to Waco, Texas.

Although their paths may have crossed in Texas, they both ended up in Ben Pollack's band.

Dave Matthews had a reputation for being a versatile, dependable sax player. Best known for his skills as a lead alto player. However, Dave played tenor very much in the style of Ben Webster.

Matthews was the first musician James hired for the new band. They had followed similar paths in their Big Band careers at that point. Matthews had played with Ben Pollack, Benny Goodman, and the Jimmy Dorsey bands before accepting Harry's offer to join his new band.

It has always been a curiosity to me that Harry hired Matthews to play lead alto.

Harry had loved Herschel Evans' sound on tenor sax. Evans played a lyrical, breathy Webster/Hawkins approach on his tenor sax solos.

That was precisely the sound that Dave Matthews played on tenor sax.

However, James already had a tenor soloist in mind.

Claude Lakey.

Lakey hailed from Nacogdoches, Texas. A scant two hours from James' home of Beaumont.

Doubtless, their paths had crossed. When James offered Claude a job, Lakey was glad to accept. Claude Lakey had been playing the second alto with Glenn Miller. Not often getting a solo spotlight with Miller, James promised him opportunities to record solos.

Claude Lakey was well known as a versatile musician. Lakey played lead alto, tenor sax, and with James, could be the fifth trumpet when needed. He was also an excellent arranger, and along with Matthews, could not only write charts but could do the task of the copyist for Harry's occasional composing. (Harry was a notoriously sloppy writer)

Claude Lakey was the copyist for Harry's composition "Flash," which remained in the book for many years. He was listed as the co-author, along with Harry.

Another fellow Texan was Drew Page. Page was a journeyman saxophonist who played with many of the Big Bands and had a long career.

In his book "Drew's Blues," Page relates seeing a skinny, thirteen-year-old Harry James working with musicians much older than him and playing great. That was in 1928.

Page also spoke highly about Harry's humility, which never diminished throughout his life.

Harry James felt good about his choices for the trumpet section in his new band. Tommy Gonsulin, a veteran of the Krupa, and Teagarden bands; Claude Bowen played with many of the major bands, including Shaw, Miller, and both Dorseys.

The third addition to the new trumpet section was Jack Palmer. Palmer was a New Yorker, whose resume included Larry Clinton, Red Norvo and Jan Savitt. Palmer was well known as a big-toned jazz soloist. So, when Harry offered him a job, he warned that

Palmer wouldn't get much of an opportunity to play trumpet solos.

Palmer replied that was alright with him, "I don't mind, he said, I love to hear YOU play Harry!"

The trombone section on day one, was Russell Brown and Truett Jones, both from Texas.

"Jumbo" Jack Gardner was hired to play piano and add some novelty vocals. On guitar was Bryan "Red" Kent, and on bass Thurman Teague, both from Texas.

Harry approached young Buddy Rich to play drums. Rich turned him down, as he was moving up in the Big Band world, destined to leave Artie Shaw to join Tommy Dorsey.

James would continue to pursue Rich for the next twenty-five years obsessively.

Harry hired Ralph Hawkins as the James band drummer. Not much is known about Hawkins, other than he also played briefly with Artie Shaw's band, and that he was a bit of sarcastic wit. Hawkins' sarcasm raised the ire of band vocalist Frank Sinatra on at least one occasion.

Next came the arrangers.

Harry immediately commissioned Andy Gibson to write about a dozen arrangements for the band.

Gibson had written for literally all the "black bands" of the era, including Ellington and Basie. Also, he had written some memorable charts for Charlie Barnet, who shared James's love for Ellington.

In addition to the arrangements Gibson had submitted, Dave Matthews, Claude Lakey, and Harry himself had written the remainder of the then existent James book. The band also had several "head arrangements," A few of which eventually were submitted on paper and stayed in the James book.

Dave Matthews's arrangement of "King Porter Stomp" remained in the book for twenty years.

The arrangements that the young Harry James band played were intended to emulate Ellington, Basie, and Lunceford.

The last necessity for any big band of the day, particularly if they were playing for dancers, was a female vocalist.

The first female vocalist that Harry hired was a lady named Beatrice Byers. Her voice was unremarkable, and her delivery was in a quite nasal tone. She lasted less than three months with Harry's new band. She did record several vocals with the band, some of which were among the few unmemorable records of Harry's career.

In May, a very young lady named Yvonne Marie Antoinette Jasme was auditioning all over New York City. Her mother was suggesting people and places take her daughter for auditions.

Harry hired her for $40 a week. One condition would be that she change her name. Harry suggested "Connie Ames" however she settled on Connie Haines.

Connie brought a new enthusiasm to the struggling James band. Her Southern accent showed she was from Georgia, and her powerful, if youthful voice, enabled her to deliver songs with a style much like Mildred Bailey and Helen Humes.

During the early days of Harry's new Orchestra, several recordings were made that have had lasting significance.

Although there were times that Harry actively emulated Louis Armstrong in some of his recordings, it was evident that there was no other player like Harry James.

"I'm in the Market for You" had been recorded by Louis Armstrong in 1930. Dave Matthews wrote an arrangement that leaned heavily on Armstrong's record. The James band recorded "Market" three times. In 1939 for Columbia, 1941, for World Transcription Services in 1941 and again in 1962 for MGM.

The Columbia record from 1939, featured a muted James. The comparisons to Armstrong are inevitable. While on the Columbia record, James does not soar into the upper range of the trumpet, as did Armstrong, James did utilize the extended range on the two subsequent recordings.

The significant differences between Louis Armstrong and Harry James were a combination of masterful technique and Harry's superior familiarity with harmonics and the chord structure. Throughout his entire career, Harry James exhibited the ability to improvise using the whole chord. Rather than just playing melody, he bobbed and weaved throughout all the notes in the chord structure of every tune.

It was this innate sense of harmonics that set Harry James' ballad playing apart from all other trumpet players of the era.

Another recording of lasting significance was recorded during the James band's first session. On February 20, 1939, along with the James theme "Ciribiribin," they recorded Dave Matthews's arrangement of "Sweet Georgia Brown."

Compared with most of the Big Band recordings from 1939, "Sweet Georgia Brown" was a "Tour de Force" for the whole James band.

Starting with Harry's opening four bars into Jack Gardner's Barrelhouse piano chorus, all at a pace that is rocking.

Then Harry takes a relatively subdued muted solo.

Dave Matthews takes an alto sax solo that Johnny Hodges-like.

The highlights continue with the first of many "Trumpet Section soli" passages led by Harry himself. The intricate trumpet section portion of "Georgia" set the stage for the next three decades, with Harry and the trumpet section playing passages which would be the envy of many prominent band leaders.

"Sweet Georgia Brown" also perfectly illustrates a problem that Harry began having with his new band. The trumpet parts were written with Harry James in mind. Parts not efficiently executed by the trumpet sections of the day.

The result was that Harry James had to play lead trumpet AND play all the solos.

Exhausting even for someone of Harry James' strength.

Enter Donald S. Reinhardt!

Donald S. Reinhardt

It is not known how and where Harry James and Donald Reinhardt first met.

Reinhardt had moved from Philadelphia to New York City, intending to be a trumpet instructor. Even in 1939, New York was a tough place to start teaching students.

Harry asked Reinhardt to come to the Ben Franklin Hotel, where the James band was performing, to listen to his brass players.

After the first set, Harry asked Donald Reinhardt to give his opinions about the quality of the James brass sections. When Reinhardt had given his critique, James asked him to do some coaching for his musicians.

Although Reinhardt could not lift the trumpet players to Harry's level, he did improve some techniques.

It was apparent that there was nothing that Reinhardt could teach Harry James, however, there were some things that Reinhardt needed to know more about from Harry James.

However, it happened, Harry James had utterly mastered the trumpet by the age of twenty-four years old. As Joe Graves and several other trumpet players have said through the years, there was nothing that Harry couldn't play on a trumpet.

Harry himself told me that he could play anything that he could think.

Harry James utilized two scarce and difficult skills when he played.

First was Harry's fantastic use of alternate fingerings.

Alternate fingerings may be used to improve facility in specific passages, making seemingly impossible phrases easier to execute.

To this day, I hear comments from modern generation trumpet players, express amazement at watching a video where Harry executes a phrase that remains mind-boggling.

The other skill that Harry used was the use of the trumpet's "Air Chambers."

Today if you ask most trumpet players to define "Air Chambers," you might get a blank expression.

Donald Reinhardt later taught his students and wrote this explanation of the "Air Chamber" concept.

"When speaking of an air chamber, we are referring to the seven original chromatic finger combinations used to descend from low C to low F sharp: (0)-(2)-(1) -(1-2) -(2-3) -(1-3)-(1-2-3). Starting from any open tone on the instrument and descending six semitones (halftones) using the above finger combinations in the same order constitutes one air chamber.

If this fingering is used to descend chromatically from all open tones on your instrument, every possible finger combination will be covered. With the exception that the tones produced by the (1-2) finger combination can be played (3)".

Using this technique can produce intonation problems with some notes, necessitating the use of the first and third valve slides to fine-tune the notes.

Harry never used the first and third valve slides. In fact, his custom-made King trumpets didn't even have slide rings.

Harry always tuned with his chops. And he still played in tune.

Reinhardt marveled at seeing and hearing this young trumpet master throw off technical passages that were nearly impossible.

All of this influenced the teaching of Donald S. Reinhardt for the rest of his life.

Harry asked him how many trumpet students Donald Reinhardt had.

Reinhardt answered, "Two."

Here is Donald S. Reinhardt's retelling of the story.

Reinhardt: "In 1939, I was the instructor of the Harry James Brass Section, even though I never

had him personally as a student. For several months in the Benjamin Franklin Hotel,

his band rehearsed with closed doors. He took the band on the road and asked me to

come to the Steel Pier, in Atlantic City, after the first few weeks to see if the brass

section had improved while on the road. He was happy with my work and suggested that

I start a teaching school in New York. I finally went to New York on Sundays only. On three Sundays, I was only able to get two students - not enough to even pay for my train fare. At that time, the James Band was coming from the Steel Pier, in Atlantic City, to the Astor Hotel in New York.

When they arrived, I went over to say hello to the guys and Harry. I told Harry that

"Laid an Egg In New York" and was going to forget the whole episode. He asked me

who were the two students and I told him the second trumpet from the CBS Studio Band.

And the first trombone from the NBC Studio Band. He stated: "my God, man, you do start at the top, don't you"? I told him that I was charging the standard 1940 New York

teaching price of $5.00 per half hour. He immediately asked me what I would think

happened to his band when coming to New York from Atlantic City. I told him that I did

not know, and he stated that the price of his band doubled when coming to New York

because in New York, it had to be expensive, or it could not be good. He stated that I

should charge $15. 00 a lesson and state no length of time for it. His drummer was a

sign painter, and he made a small sign stating my $15. 00 a lesson price and that I was

only in New York on Sundays."

Harry still had to play most of the lead trumpet parts, but Donald S. Reinhardt was given his place in trumpet history!

Three weeks after the James band's first recording session, Harry led the band into the studio once again to cut two sides.

The first tune was "'Tain't What You Do (It's the Way That You Do It)" featuring trumpeter Jack Palmer on the vocal. The song had been a hit recording for Jimmie Lunceford with trombonist Trummy Young on vocals. However, the Andy Gibson arrangement leaned more to the Count Basie sound.

The "B' side was "Two O' Clock Jump." "Jump" had its birth in the Benny Goodman trumpet section.

"One O' Clock Jump," which began as a "head" arrangement in Count Basie. Benny Goodman added it to his repertoire in 1937.

After the Goodman band had recorded it on January 21, 1937, the constant repetition of one-night stands, brought about changes created in the minds of the Goodman trumpet section.

One night, Harry suggested to his battery mates that they should add some triplets during the ride out of "One O' Clock Jump".

Those triplets followed Harry James into the studio on March 6, 1939.

The James-added triplets, along with the trumpet solo at the opening of the tune, warranted James being added as co-composer, along with Goodman and Basie to the "Two O' Clock Jump."

Along with "You Made Me Love You," no tune was more identified with Harry James as "Two O' Clock Jump."

During the next 44 years, Harry and the band recorded "Jump" eight different times, all with different arrangements.

Sinatra

Frank Sinatra was obsessed with being a singing star.

He would sing anywhere, for anyone who would listen. He paid for a demo record of "Our Love" at a local studio out of his own pocket. He also auditioned for a spot with Bob Chester's new band in March of 1939.

Sinatra took a job as a singing waiter at a roadside club in New Jersey called "The Rustic Cabin."

The job didn't pay well. However, Frank knew they had a telephone line hookup to New York's famed radio giant WNEW.

One night in late-May of 1939, Louise Tobin, who was married to Harry James at the time, was listening to the WNEW broadcast from the "Rustic Cabin." She heard a pleasant, very musical male vocalist singing on the radio.

Tobin suggested to Harry James that he should listen to the singer.

James had been napping when Louise called attention to the radio. James had barely listened to the youthful singer when he called his manager Jerry Barrett.

James and Barrett took a cab across the bridge to New Jersey. The story goes that James asked the doorman where the singer was. He was told that they didn't have a singer, but they did have a waiter who sang a little bit.

According to Sinatra, when he was told that Harry James was there to hear him, he ripped off his apron and pushed the piano to the middle of the dance floor.

He convinced the house band pianist to play "Night and Day."

When he had finished his song, James approached him and offered him a job for $75 a week.

Since Sinatra was making about $20 a week, he jumped at the chance to sing with the new Harry James Orchestra.

He rejected Harry's attempts to have Frank change his last name to "Satin."

It was known from the beginning that Frank Sinatra wanted to sing romantic ballads.

However, as great as Andy Gibson and Dave Matthews were as arrangers, writing charts for romantic ballads was not their strong suit. Harry needed to find an arranger that could deliver lush ballad arrangements for his young singing star.

There is surprisingly very little information about Jack Mathias. He had been the piano player in a band led by Jerry Blaine from 1937-1938. He ghost-wrote some arrangements for Henry Mancini in the sixties.

It is also unknown just how the paths of Jack Mathias and Harry James crossed. However, in the Fall of 1939, Jack Mathias wrote some charts for James and Sinatra.

The first chart Mathias provided was of a new song called "All or Nothing at All," which had come to Harry James by way of a publisher/song plugger named Lou Levy. The song was only a minor hit for Jimmy Dorsey and his Orchestra, featuring Bob Eberle.

The James record of "All or Nothing at All," was different from every other tune that Harry James and his Orchestra had to date played. But it did portend of the future song selections in the career of Harry James.

The first seven notes played, told everyone in the record-buying public whose band it was. Rather than having a piano intro, or even a complicated band introduction, it was merely the golden trumpet of Harry James, playing the first seven notes as though it was a fanfare. The full band only gave Harry a supportive base over which he could deliver his musical business card.

As if to say, "Ladies and Gentlemen, here is Harry James"!

The band settles down quickly, leaving Frank Sinatra a quiet cushion on which he delivered the lyrics, in an entirely new style. Neither Bob Eberle, nor his brother Ray Eberly, nor Jack Leonard, or any other male vocalist sang like Sinatra. Not even Bing Crosby could emote in such an emotional, vulnerable fashion.

Then as Sinatra finishes his chorus, Harry James majestically rises above the band as the lead trumpet to lead to the Sinatra climax!

The only problem was the record was a flop. It only sold 8000 copies. It certainly was not the fault of Frank or Harry.

Columbia Records had gotten wind of the complaints from night club owners. The Harry James Orchestra was officially the "loudest band in the land." It was challenging to pitch woo, or even hold a civil conversation in a room where Harry and his boys held court.

Columbia Records began to cut their losses and cut Harry James from the label.

And that didn't make Frank Sinatra very happy!

On November 8, 1939, Frank Sinatra recorded the last of his side with the Harry James Orchestra.

"Every Day of My Life" listed Harry James as a co-writer. It featured trombonist Truett Jones in an entire chorus. The Jack Mathias arrangement gives yet more examples of the superb lead trumpet playing of Harry James.

The same session produced the recording of both James and Sinatra named as perhaps the worst recording of their careers..." Ciribiribin" featuring a Sinatra vocal.

To be fair, the performance is not that bad. It's just that the "Americanized" lyrics written for the recording were awful. Besides, Sinatra had not yet developed his swing chops and was uncomfortable in the swing setting written by Andy Gibson.

The recording did provide another showcase of James' total mastery of the trumpet. This ability would be displayed in an even more excellent way in the next James recording session.

The James band also recorded Harry James' composition "Flash" in this session. "Flash" had been a "head arrangement" from the beginning of the James band.

Jack Mathias finally put "Flash" on music paper.

Artie Shaw had released his recording of "Lady Be Good" in early 1939. The James band's record of "Flash" was based on the chord changes of "Lady," and Harry borrowed some of the riffs from the Shaw version.

"Flash" stayed in the James band book for two decades. It was most recognized as a feature for Buddy Rich in the album Harry James at the Hollywood Palladium in 1954.

Three weeks later, on November 30th, the Harry James Orchestra returned to the Columbia studio for the last time for over a year.

The band recorded four sides. They were "I'm in the Market for You," "Night Special," "Concerto for Trumpet," and "Back Beat Boogie."

"Back Beat Boogie" was another "head arrangement" that was in the James band repertoire from day one. Again, Jack Mathias put to paper the combination of Harry's original composition and the riffs that the band had added during ten months of performance.

Much like "Two O' Clock Jump," "Back Beat Boogie" stayed in the James performing library for the next thirty years. The tune changed over the years, and still retained the elements of adding riffs, and section parts during performances.

As I write these pages in 2020, "Concerto for Trumpet" has become played by trumpet players all over the World. Once thought of as too difficult by many players to even attempt.

Harry had written "Concerto for Trumpet" with help from Jack Mathias.

I once asked Harry how "Concerto" came about. He told me that "Flight of the Bumblebee" was something that he had played since he was a teenager. The idea for "Concerto" had come from telling some musicians, that "Bumblebee" was so easy for him, that he could play it backward, and upside down.

So essentially, the first part of "Concerto for Trumpet" was actually "Bumblebee" upside down. He added a nod to "Sing, Sing, Sing" in the midsection. And then the last chorus is based on the Herbert L. Clarke arrangement of "Carnival of Venice."

Harry only performed "Concerto for Trumpet" a handful of times. Including in the 1942 motion picture "Private Buckaroo."

As one door closes

Back in January 1939, well Frank Sinatra was auditioning for the Bob Chester band, Tommy Dorsey happened to be eavesdropping.

At that point in time, Tommy Dorsey had begun to look for a replacement for his vocalist Jack Leonard. Although Leonard hadn't given notice at that point, Dorsey had some anxiety about losing Leonard, leaving him without a star vocalist.

Tommy Dorsey couldn't very well hire Frank Sinatra while Jack Leonard was still with the band. So, Tommy Dorsey passed on hiring Sinatra at that time. But he found a way the name Frank Sinatra in his mind for further use.

While Frank Sinatra had given his notice to Harry James, Jack Leonard gave his notice to Tommy Dorsey. Leonard's immediate replacement was Alan DeWitt. However, DeWitt only lasted about three weeks, giving Tommy Dorsey enough time to snatch up the free agent Frank Sinatra.

By November of 1939, Harry had lost a little confidence in his long-term success as a bandleader. When Sinatra tendered his notice to Harry, Harry quipped that since Tommy Dorsey was doing so well, maybe James himself might ask Dorsey for a job.

Harry instructed his manager Jerry Barrett to tear up Frank Sinatra's contract period even though six months were remaining on it. The breakup was amicable, and Harry and Sinatra remained friends for life.

Harry James was in no hurry to replace Sinatra. He was having enough trouble making payroll and keeping Connie Haines aboard.

Meanwhile, while the Harry James Orchestra struggled to gain a foothold in the with the public, Harry himself was still the fan favorite as a trumpet soloist.

On February 7, 1940, Harry had again won the Metronome reader's poll as Best Trumpet soloist. Harry took part in a memorable recording session with the Metronome All-Stars.

There were several reasons the session was memorable. For one, the guitarist was Charlie Christian. As a member of the Benny Goodman Orchestra, Christian was already recognized as an agent of change in Jazz history.

Though only twenty-four years old, he was a fundamental part of the soon to emerge "Bebop" genre. His improvisational lines became legendary. Being born the same year as Dizzy Gillespie, Christian came to the forefront of Jazz while Dizzy was trying to find his musical voice.

The first side recorded at the Metronome session was the Fletcher Henderson arrangement of "King Porter Stomp." Harry played the opening solo, as he had countless times was Goodman, and Ziggy Elman played the second trumpet solo.

The most memorable side was the tune "All-Star Strut." "Strut" was played by a combination of musicians called "The All-Star Nine."

The nine musicians chose by Metronome magazine, were indeed the top players on their respective instruments.

The group included Benny Goodman on clarinet, Jack Teagarden on trombone, Benny Carter on alto sax, Eddie Miller on tenor sax, Jess Stacy on piano, Bob Haggart on bass, Charlie Christian on guitar, Gene Krupa on drums, and Harry James as the trumpet soloist.

A hastily arranged "head" chart based on twelve-bar blues, "Strut" featured each soloist, and once again proved Harry James' superiority as a leader and soloist.

In February of 1940, Harry made some changes in the personnel of his band. Some by attrition, with players leaving for better-paying gigs. Harry released others as he was trying to find his way in the maze of Popular Music.

One significant change had occurred when Ralph Hawkins left the drum position in November of 1939. Mickey Scrima replaced him.

Scrima had a reputation as a loud drummer, with a personality to match.

In a 1977 interview on a retrospective of the Harry James band on Merv Griffin's show, Dick Haymes described Mickey Scrima.

"He had a very bad temper...and every time he'd lose his temper, he'd start playing louder and louder. And his bass drum was right behind my head. Buddy Rich was quite confidential compared to that guy!"

Other changes in the James band included Ben Heller joining as a guitarist, Vido Musso as tenor sax soloist, (moving Claude Lakey to alto sax) and adding Chuck Gentry on baritone sax.

Perhaps the most significant change came when Jack Schaeffer left the trumpet section

When Harry hired Schaeffer, James finally got a lead trumpet player!

The Other Count

Dominick "Nick" Buono began playing trumpet in his native San Diego, California, by the age of eleven. He was quite well-known in the Italian American community.

In the late thirties, Buono had played lead trumpet for several bands, including the bands of Sonny Dunham, and Vido Musso.

One night in late 1939, Musso's band was playing the Panther Room of the Hotel Sherman in Chicago. The band was being fronted by Johnny "Scat" Davis, with whom Harry had crossed paths during the filming of the "Hollywood Hotel" with Benny Goodman in 1937.

Harry had gone to hear Vido Musso. However, his attention was drawn to the lead trumpet player, Nick Buono. Harry was impressed by his bright, full tone, and by his professionalism on the bandstand.

Harry offered Buono a job. Although the James band was struggling to find success, it would be a step up in Nick Buono's career.

Harry began immediately to call Nick Buono the "Count." Because of his regal presence. Harry thought Nick looked like a European nobleman, a Count!

Nick was forever called "Count."

Nick's effect on the James band was immediate. His lead trumpet skills freed Harry up to play his solos and front the band much more.

Nick Buono was also a positive influence on his fellow musicians. He was a funny guy, with a bent toward practical jokes.

Nick was well known for his cooking...Italian Style.

Over the many years that Nick Buono was with the Harry James Orchestra, Nick would find ways to cook in his hotel room. Big Italian meals were prepared for himself and anybody else who cared to enjoy his cuisine. Lasagna was his specialty.

Not any easy meal to create in a motel room, without a kitchen!

Sal Monte used to tell his favorite "Count" Buono kitchen incident:

(I've heard this story from several people, including former James band member Fred Radke)

"Nick never ate in restaurants while on the road. He would always cook pasta in his room, and one night when he left to go to the gig, he forgot to turn off the steamer that made his pasta, and when he returned, all of the wallpaper in the hotel room was peeled off the wall.

When Sal got ready to pay the hotel bill, the hotel manager said, and that will be $2000 extra to refurbish the room that one of your band Members destroyed!

Sal went to Harry and asked how do you want to handle this. Harry laughed and said: "Pay it!"

I got to witness Nick's brand of humor many years later.

In September of 1979, I had driven St Louis to see the James band for two nights.

The second morning that I was in St Louis, I had taken three members of Harry's band on a tour of St. Louis in my car.

When I took them back to their hotel, we arrived in time to see the "Count" running from room to room, outside, in his boxer shorts. He had filled his bucket with ice and hit the ice jackpot.

The machine would not stop cranking out ice, so Nick didn't want to see all that ice wasted. He was running from door to door, asking for empty ice buckets!

Nick Buono spent most of the next 43 years in the James trumpet section. He would leave for short time-outs, always to return to the band.

The last time I saw Harry James was June 10, 1983. He was terminally ill but continued to front his famous Big Band.

There in the trumpet section, was the "Count."

I got to spend some time with Nick Buono between sets. He was anxious at the prospect of "losing his gig" with Harry. Nick asked me if there were any Big Band gigs, I would recommend to him.

Nick told me how, from 1940 until 1983, he had gradually moved down in the trumpet section. Beginning as the first trumpet player, eventually moving down to the fourth trumpet.

Nick had played the James book for so long that he didn't need the sheet music. He would sometimes sit on the fourth trumpet book, not needing to refer to it.

James and Haymes

In January 1940, Harry replaced Frank Sinatra with a Canadian vocalist named Fran Heines.

From the beginning, James did not like the sound of Heines' voice, and Heines was given his walking papers after about two weeks.

At the same time, Harry was rehearsing the band at the famed NOLA Rehearsal studio on W 57th Street in New York City.

Larry Shayne was a songwriter/song plugger in New York.

One afternoon, Shayne brought in a young songwriter to play his songs for Harry James.

In the 1977 interview on the Merv Griffin Show, Haymes related his version of the meeting:

"I was writing some bad songs. Harry was rehearsing the band at NOLA Studios in New York. And I heard 'Gee the new Harry James was rehearsing up at NOLA Studio' and I figured I'd go up and tout my songs. When I got up there, and Harry's rehearsal was over, I sat down very nervously and started playing, and singing my songs in the only key I could play in.

Harry hated the songs, but he hired me right then and there, as the singer with the band".

Dick Haymes recorded his first sides with the Harry James Orchestra on March 18, 1940. They were "You've Got Me Out on a Limb," and "How High the Moon."

By this time, the James recordings were for Varsity Records. Varsity was a relatively "minor league" label, and the early records by James and Haymes were not very successful.

Eli Oberstein was a record producer and former RCA executive, who is mostly responsible for creating the RCA Bluebird. After leaving RCA, Oberstein started three new record labels. Crown and Royale, which both flopped. And Varsity Records.

In the beginning, Oberstein was able to attract attention to Varsity upon the promise of luring away major recording artists from RCA/Bluebird.

The best Oberstein could get for the Varsity label, were largely small-time entertainers and bands. At least at the time.

Oberstein signed Harry James to a contract. He also suggested to Harry that he should make a recording of "The Flight of the Bumblebee."

Written by Nikolai Rimsky-Korsakov as a piece in an opera, was best known as a violin feature.

Oberstein thought that if Harry James could play a trumpet version, it would be a recording first, and a hit.

Harry wrote the original arrangement of "Bumblebee" himself. It featured a "swing" portion in the performance.

It was the best example of Harry's masterful, classical training.

The initial recording of "Flight of the Bumblebee" was not a huge commercial success. But it became one of the tunes most requested by Harry James fans for the next three decades.

Harry subsequently recorded "The Flight of the Bumblebee" three other times.

On February 13, 1941, Harry recorded "Bumblebee" with the addition of a string quartet, this time in a Jack Mathias arrangement.

The band recorded "Bumblebee" in May of 1941 for the World Transcription Services.

A word about the World Transcription Services. "World" recorded for V-Disc and radio broadcast uses. The fidelity from the "World Transcription Service" studios, was somewhat superior to what the capabilities of the commercial record companies at the time.

Several of the James recordings for "World" provided records that were not commercially available in those days. They later surfaced in the 1970s and provided fans to finally own these technically superior versions of Harry's early recordings.

An interesting record was made for "World" during the sessions that produced "Bumblebee" and "Carnival of Venice."

Dick Haymes could perform his version of "All or Nothing at All," using the same arrangement recorded by Frank Sinatra.

The record demonstrated the stark differences between the voices of Haymes and Sinatra.

Dick Haymes had a classic rich, baritone voice. His mother was an opera teacher.

Sinatra showed a softer, more emotional approach that became a hallmark of his entire career.

Harry James returned to "The Flight of the Bumblebee: during a "live" recording by Columbia Records on October 25, 1952. It was released as "One Night Stand" from the Aragon Ballroom in Chicago.

A decidedly different approach to "Bumblebee" featured a duet with Harry and Tommy Gumina on accordion. The band only came in for the last note.

Harry James and his Orchestra performed "Flight of the Bumblebee" on The Ed Sullivan Show, on March 16, 1953. They played it again in December of 1953, on a television show called "Chance of a Lifetime."

"The Flight of the Bumblebee" again resurfaced in a broadcast of "The Big Record" hosted by Patti Page on November 13, 1957.

Harry reprised a short version of "Bumblebee" on an episode of the Danny Tomas Show in 1963. In that episode, Harry had an acting part as a YMCA music instructor.

Although he had several acting parts in Hollywood movies, the "Thomas" show demonstrated perhaps the most realistic acting performance of his career.

He starts a tune with the Earle Hagen studio orchestra with a quote of "Bumblebee" and leads into a wild solo on a blues number. The episode ends with Harry and young Rusty Hamer on drums, in a recreation of Harry's solo from "Sing, Sing, Sing."

I saw Harry play "The Flight of the Bumblebee" once during a dance engagement of the James band during the late 1970s

A local high school band director has brought some of the students from his band to see Harry James. After the end of the band's first set. Harry headed to the bar.

A teenage trumpet player stopped Harry dead in his tracks, and asked "Hey Harry, can you still play Flight of the Bumblebee?

Harry looked down at the kid with those bright, blue eyes.

He replied, "I can play it if you can dance to it!"

When the band returned to the stand, he called up "The Flight of the Bumblebee."

Harry played one chorus, flawlessly.

The teenage trumpet player proceeded to flail, alone on the dance floor.

After the set, Harry walked up to the bar and ordered a Coke.

He delivered the Coke to the breathless young man.

"Now, if you asked respectfully, next time you won't look so stupid, kid!"

On the February 13, 1941, session, Harry and the band recorded four classically rooted pieces. In addition to "The Flight of the Bumblebee," they recorded "Trumpet Rhapsody parts 1 & 2," "Chopin Waltz in C Sharp Minor," which were never released, for whatever reason.

Harry did perform "Chopin Waltz in C Sharp Minor" on a broadcast of the Chamber Music of Lower Basin Street radio broadcast on May 12, 1941.

The other classical piece was Harry's version of "The Carnival of Venice."

For trumpet players all over the world for the past hundred years, "Carnival of Venice" is nearly inescapable. It has been published in many trumpet methods, including the trumpet method carrying Harry James's name.

Harry began playing it from the strenuous lessons from his father Everette, using the famed Arban's Complete Conservatory Method for Trumpet. The Arban's book is the most revered, and most hated of all teaching methods for trumpet players.

Jean-Baptiste Arban was a 19th-century cornetist, who was the father of modern trumpet pedagogy. Virtually every professional trumpet player since 1890, at least, began their musical education in an Arban book.

Harry James often described his father requiring young Harry to learn and perfect Arban technical exercises before he could play baseball with the kids on the block.

Harry was able to take the Arban's version of "The Carnival of Venice, combine it with a "swing interpretation of the tune, and finish with his own exciting and original finale.

Harry James and his Orchestra also recorded "Carnival of Venice" for World Transcription Service in May of 1941.

To my ears, the World Transcription Service recording of "Carnival of Venice" is the superior version of the James arrangement. It was better recorded, and Harry's improvised solo was much more adventurous than the Columbia version.

During the recording session on January 22, 1941, the band also recorded a Dick Haymes vocal version of "Ol' Man River." To be sure, Dave Matthew's arrangement of "River" was somewhat erratic and took the song away from its original interpretation.

"Ol' Man River" just doesn't work as a pure "Swing" tune. However, the record did serve to introduce Dick Haymes to the listening public.

No male vocalist of the "Swing Era" had a voice like Dick Haymes. Not Sinatra, not Bob Eberle, nobody. What Dick Haymes lacked in emotional authenticity, he had in spades in sheer vocal pipes.

Dick Haymes's voice fell somewhere between Frank Sinatra and Mario Lanza!

Haymes recorded several other recordings as the male vocalist for Harry James. James and Haymes parted ways at the end of 1941. Dick Haymes left and joined Benny Goodman after Harry fired him for some unknown reason.

He lasted just three months with Goodman, after enduring Goodman noodling behind his ballad vocals.

In September of 1942, Dick Haymes replaced Frank Sinatra as vocalist for Tommy Dorsey and his Orchestra.

Schmaltz

"Schmaltz" -Definition of schmaltz

1: sentimental or florid music or art

2: sentimentality

Harry James defined schmaltz this way in a 1977 interview,

"I don't like that word. I think it's sincerity. To me, it's how you feel about performing a song. You play one song one way, and another song another way. I try to play a song as I feel it. My mother used to tell me, 'Son, why don't you play a song as I sing it?' I guess subconsciously, I thought of my Mother and how she used to sing, the first time I played "You Made Me Love You."

Whether you liked Judy Garland, or you didn't, she had an almost "magical" effect on artists. Both actors and musicians.

When Garland recorded "Dear Mr. Gable, You Made Me Love You" in the movie "Broadway Melody of 1938," Harry James, along with millions of other guys, fell under Judy's spell.

Harry James loved and defended Judy Garland until his death.

In April of 1941, when Harry James added strings to his band, he began to think about tunes he would like to play. "You Made Me Love You" nagged him like a toothache.

The song had been an enormous hit for Judy Garland, and Al Jolson. But at that time, nobody had ever recorded an instrumental version.

James had begged Columbia Records to let him record "You Made Me Love You" as Columbia continued to resist James playing anything less than Jazz-oriented.

The relationship between James and Columbia Records was still tenuous.

According to Harry himself, he wrote a sketch of an arrangement of "You Made Me Love You" in his hotel room. Harry then gave the rough score to arranger Gray Rains.

Gray Rains had just joined Harry James as a staff arranger, which now included Rains, Matthews, and Jack Mattias.

The James band had a morning recording session in New York on May 20-21, 1941, for Columbia.

Harry James recorded "You Made Me Love You" as the last tune of the session. However, Columbia sat on the recording until the next James recording on June 17, 1941.

Song plugger Larry Shayne and Mack David had brought a new song for Harry James and Dick Haymes to record. The song was "A Sinner Kissed An Angel." They were anxious to get Harry James to make a record with Haymes because they had also given to song to Tommy Dorsey and his singer Frank Sinatra.

Once again, Harry James pleaded with Columbia to release "You Made Me Love You." Finally, Columbia and James both agreed that "Sinner" was going to be such a big hit that they could safely put "You Made Me Love You" on the "B" side without affecting the success of "A Sinner Kissed An Angel."

Harry James himself explained the record in an interview with Dick Haymes and Merv Griffin in 1977.

"Well, it's very simple. We did "Sinner Kissed an Angel," and we said may we please do "You Made Me Love You," and they said we don't want that. Because Judy Garland just did it and everything else. So, we said please may we put it on the back of "Sinner Kissed an Angel," and our very dear Friend Larry Shayne wrote, "Sinner Kissed an Angel," right?

"So that's the "A" side...and all of a sudden, they're playing "You Made Me Love You."

The Harry James recording of "You Made Me Love You" debuted at Number #5 on the Billboard Charts on November b1, 1941. It remained in the Top 10 for ten weeks.

The song was forever identified with the soaring, soulful trumpet of Harry James.

And it became a source of criticism from the Jazz community.

Jazz critic Dan Morgenstern has called "You Made Me Love You" "the record that the jazz critics never forgave Harry James for recording."

However, with the record-buying public, Harry James became a star, like no other trumpet player before or since.

Trees

In March of 1983, I was privileged to spend the better part of an evening with Helen Forrest. She was proud of the fact that not only did she have an autobiography coming out, but she had recorded her first solo album in 25 years.

That night in Denver, Helen Forrest was singing as well as she ever had. Her voice was clear and strong. And the audience and dancers loved every minute of her performance.

Helen Fogel had come a long way from her birth on April 12, 1918. She had been singing with bands since she was in her teens. In 1934, she changed her name to "Forrest" because Fogel sounded too Jewish.

After having sung with the Swing Era's clarinet playing bandleaders, Artie Shaw and Benny Goodman, Helen Forrest wanted more. Helen Forrest left Artie Shaw through no fault of her own. Shaw's erratic personality and life choices sent her to Goodman.

Like Dick Haymes before her, she was too serious a singer to endure Benny's self-centeredness.

Helen was a humble person, but she was supremely confident in her singing skills.

In September of 1941, after being tipped off that Harry James was looking for a new female vocalist, she found out that James was rehearsing his band in New York City.

Harry James had just released his girl singer Lynn Richards (whom Dick Haymes described as a "dim bulb"). He was looking for a Jazz singer to replace Richards. Harry was not at all interested in a ballad singer.

In walks, Helen Forrest!

James asked what she was doing there. He knew her body of work and didn't want to be rude to her.

However, several members of the James band had worked with Forrest. They thought that she might help Harry James further success with the record-buying public.

James relented and let her sing with the band at the rehearsal.

According to Helen Forrest herself, Harry put it to a vote from the band. They voted unanimously to make Helen the new girl singer.

Many years later, Helen Forrest explained to writer George T, Simon:

"Harry James was wonderful. When I joined him, I said, 'There's only one condition: I don't care how much you pay me, I don't care about arrangements. The one thing I want is to start a chorus and finish it. I want to do verses, so don't put me up for a chorus in the middle of an instrumental.' He said, 'You got it,' and that was it."

She also told writer George T. Simon, "I'll always remain grateful to Artie and Benny. But they had been featuring me more like they did a member of the band, almost like another instrumental soloist. Harry, though, gave me just the right sort of arrangement and setting that fit a singer. It wasn't just a matter of my getting up, singing a chorus, and sitting down again." In his book, The Big Bands, Simon explained that Harry James built "the arrangements around his horn and Helen's voice. This established warmer moods by slowing down the tempo so that two, instead of the usual three or more choruses, would fill a record. Many an arrangement would build to a closing climax during Helen's vocal so that she would emerge as its star."

From the beginning, Harry called Helen "Trees" because of her last name.

With the Harry James Orchestra, Helen Forrest forever earned the title "The Voice of the Big Bands." With Harry James she had several hit recordings, including "Skylark," I Had the Craziest Dream," "Make Love to Me," "But Not for Me," "He's My Guy," "I Don't Want to Walk Without You," and her biggest hit "I've Heard That Song Before." That song caused Columbia Records to run out of the shellac needed to make their records.

Much has been written, including by Forrest herself about her relationship with Harry James. Forrest had an intimate relationship with James for three years that ended when Harry broke up with her to marry Betty Grable and said to her death that she was always in love with him.

Success at Last

From the phone call to invite Harry James to join the Benny Goodman Orchestra to the success of "You Made Me Love You," it took five years.

Not meteoric by today's media-driven standards. But a relatively short time to most of us.

Immediately songwriters and song pluggers deluged Harry James with new material. Harry's commercial success was undeniable.

High school girls put his picture in their lockers at school. Offers came for Harry to appear in motion pictures.

Virtually every night of the week, you could listen to a Harry James remote radio broadcast, regardless of where you lived in the United States.

Still, Harry never forsook his deep Jazz roots. Despite the addition of an ever-growing string section, Harry James and His Music Makers turned out many swinging records.

One of those was "The Mole," which was co-written by Harry and arranger LeRoy Holmes.

LeRoy Holmes was one of the most successful composers and arrangers from the Swing Era. He went on to great success in Hollywood. He also wrote and conducted many hit recordings until he died in 1977.

"The Mole" featured a repeated baritone sax figure that pops in and out of the string-laden ensemble. It also featured a flag-waving trumpet section passage led by Harry James. "The Mole stayed in the James book for the next forty-two years, with the strings being replaced by muted trumpets.

"The Mole" was found on the "B" side of "But Not for Me," a hit for Harry and Helen Forrest.

Another instrumental tune that stayed in the Harry James Orchestra library was "Strictly Instrumental." Written by famed composer Edgar Battle a melody, the Jack Mathias arrangement featured a back and forth between Harry James, using a cup mute on his trumpet, and the ensemble. In the third chorus, Harry begins his open trumpet chorus with a run-up to a double-high G. (This recording helped to ensure Harry's fame as a "high note" player)

The second chorus of "Strictly Instrumental" featured a tenor sax solo by the musician who replaced Vido Musso and remained in the first tenor chair for the next thirty-five years.

Corky

Gene Patrick "Corky" Corcoran was born on July 28, 1924, in Tacoma, Washington.

Corky Corcoran began playing the saxophone as a young boy and was labeled as a "Child prodigy" in his early teens. In 1940, bandleader Jimmie Lunceford heard him playing in a local band at a school dance. Aside from Corcoran's ethnicity, being a teenage white boy in an all-black ensemble was not a favorable situation, Corky was fifteen years old.

Lunceford did suggest to fellow bandleader Sonny Dunham that he should hire young Corcoran. Dunham hired him to replace former James saxophonist Dave Matthews.

From the beginning, Corky Corcoran was recognized as a virtuoso tenor sax player, whose playing caused inevitable comparisons with Ben Webster and Coleman Hawkins.

It did not take long for Corcoran to realize that Sonny Dunham's band was not a good place for a sixteen-year-old. His sudden need for an appendectomy allowed him to get out of a less than favorable situation.

It is not known for sure just how Corky Corcoran came to the attention of Harry James. However, James only needed to hear Corky play once, to realize that despite his young age, Corky Corcoran was the tenor sax player of Harry's dreams!

James hastened to pay Corcoran's medical bills and, in October of 1941, offered him a job.

Due to child-labor laws of the day and the fact that the Harry James Orchestra was on the road constantly, it caused James to become Corky's legal guardian. Contrary to many accounts over the decades, Harry did not adopt Corky as his son. He was his legal guardian, and longtime James manager Frank "Pee Wee" Monte shouldered most of those responsibilities in the beginning.

To be fair, Corcoran, even as a teenager, was a walking stereotype. He was relatively small in stature. Added to that was the fact that Corcoran was a red-haired Irish kid with a quick trigger, who early on began to assimilate the bad habits of James and some of his fellow musicians. Corky was a hard-drinking, heavy smoker, and became steadily more unstable as years went by.

Musically, Corky Corcoran's tenor sound became almost as recognizable as Harry himself. With solos on so many James recordings, such as "The Mole," "Crazy Rhythm," "Strictly Instrumental," and most notably of all, "I've Heard That Song Before" and "I'm Beginning to See the Light."

For much of the next thirty-five years, Corky Corcoran sat in the first saxophone chair. He would occasionally have too much to drink, causing him to get into fights with Harry, Monte, and whoever else who crossed his path.

In 1947, he left to join Tommy Dorsey's band. However, those two Irish tempers were incompatible.

Perhaps the finest recorded of Corky Corcoran's playing is from the "Original" Stardust by Lionel Hampton All-Stars from the "Just Jazz" Concert

Recorded Civic Auditorium, Pasadena, Calif., August 4, 1947, Corky was part of a monster group of Jazz giants.

In addition to Lionel Hampton and Corky Corcoran, was Charlie Shavers on trumpet, Willie Smith on alto, Barney Kessel on guitar, Tommy Todd on piano, Slam Stewart on bass, and Lee Young and Jackie Mills sharing the drumming responsibilities.

Corcoran could stretch out during his solos, in a way that he never had with Harry James or any other Big Band.

He would go home to Tacoma several times and start a small band, where he could play more Jazz. He recorded three albums under his name over the years.

I have often wondered what career might have happened for Corky Corcoran if he had never joined the Harry James Orchestra.

Inevitably though, he would return to the Harry James Orchestra. Musically, Corky Corcoran and Harry James were a perfect match.

The last time I saw talked to Corky was in February of 1973. He was excited because he was getting married and had a new album coming out. He asked for my mailing address, and a month later, I received two copies of Corky's album called "Corky Corcoran plays Something."

Corky Corcoran died of cancer on October 4, 1979. My Wife, Cheryl Morris, who was the James band vocalist at that time, was the person called upon to inform Harry.

Harry James did not take it well.

Good Times

I have come to believe that there have been, and are many excellent musicians, who are not entertainers. I think perhaps that someday, scientists will discover that there is an "Entertainer Gene" in the DNA of many people.

Harry James had the "Entertainer Gene" for sure.

He was a consummate showman. He understood the pulse of dancers. This gave him an innate ability to select tempos that were appropriate for dancers. He also knew how to put on a show that endeared him to audiences for forty-four years.

By 1942, three years after he started his band, Harry James was at the top of the Music and Entertainment business. His records were selling incredibly well. His public appearances were invariably sold-out.

In February of 1942, Harry James and his Orchestra recorded two sides that were to demonstrate the course that Harry James had set for the remainder of his career.

In 1930, British composer Eric Coates wrote light-orchestral waltz entitled "By the Sleepy Lagoon." In 1940, American songwriter Jack Lawrence wrote a set of lyrics that became embroiled for two years in copyright and artistic license issues.

In February of 1942, Lawrence brought the song to Harry James. James immediately recognized the melody's value. But as he frequently did with songwriters in his career, he told them that he needed to change the original delivery of the song to suit his trumpet and his dancing public.

Harry James performed very few waltz-tempo songs in his career. "Sleepy Lagoon" needed to be delivered with a romantic fox-trot delivery.

As usual, James was one hundred percent correct!

Jack Mathias lifted the introduction from Ravel's "Daphnis et Chloé, Suite No. 2", and placed it over a bed of strings. This intro ushered in a Harry James solo that continues to give listeners goosebumps nearly eighty years later.

James plays the melody with masterful control and incredible emotional intensity. After which there is a string section passage.

This was followed by a trombone solo by Hoyt Bohannon, whose fame is second only perhaps to Milt Bernhart's legendary solo in the Nelson Riddle-Frank Sinatra recording of "I've Got You Under My Skin."

(Bohannon's solo on "Sleepy Lagoon" is not an easy solo for a trombonist to execute. When Harry re-recorded it for Capitol Records in 1955, he brought Hoyt Bohannon back to recreate his solo!)

"Sleepy" finishes with a high-register flourish that Harry repeated thousands of times for the rest of his life.

The "B" side of "Sleepy Lagoon" was a Harry James-Jack Mathias composition that also became a permanent addition to the James band performances until the end of Harry's life.

The title "Trumpet Blues" was used by many soloists and Big Bands over the years. However, The James recording of "Trumpet Blues" stands alone in brass history.

The word "Cantabile" is an Italian word meaning "Like a Song" or "Singable."

The Columbia recording label read "Trumpet Blues and Cantabile" because the middle section was a very lyrical passage. It perfectly demonstrated the musical mind of Harry James. It also illustrated the dichotomy in the path to commercial success that would lead Harry James for his entire career.

The piece opens with a fanfare from the Harry James-led trumpet section. As the melody is unfolded, the Harry James sound is unmistakable. If you listen closely, there are a couple of fast tongued licks that are nearly impossible. Yet James tosses them off in a "Matter of fact" manner.

The blues portion is a trumpet "tour de force" with the trumpet section playing like musical Siamese quintuplets!

The string section leads Harry and the band into a very lyrical section in which Harry's beautiful lead sound is almost mesmerizing in its delivery.

After the "Cantabile" has ended, the trumpets play a "Bugle Call" break, and finish with a flurry of hi notes, climaxing with the three sets of triplets, all tongued. And then the high E flat.

Harry played lead throughout the entire recording.

The original Columbia recording of "Trumpet Blues" was probably played at the slowest tempo that Harry and the band ever played. Over the years, there were many audio and video examples of the James band playing "Trumpet Blues." Each performance is played much faster than the original.

The tune was featured in the 1944 movie "Bathing Beauty" and in several television broadcasts over the years.

The 1955 Capitol album "Harry James in Hi-Fi" included "Trumpet Blues." On that recording, Harry shares the leadership responsibilities with the great Conrad Gozzo. The Capitol recording is the best studio recording of "Trumpet Blues."

Harry continued to perform "Trumpet Blues" in concerts up until the early 1980s.

As Harry James' fame increased, he got an offer to appear in his first Hollywood movie.

On May 28, 1942, the film "Private Buckaroo" was released to theaters. It is reasonable to conclude that some of the film's production likely began in late 1941.

"Private Buckaroo" starred not only Harry James and his Orchestra, but also The Andrews Sisters, Dick Foran, Shemp Howard, Huntz Hall, and a very young Donald O'Connor.

The plot was thin, and the production was done hurriedly on a low budget by Universal Studios in Hollywood.

The entire Harry James band gets drafted, all at the same time. The thin plot details the boot camp adventures of the cast. Harry has several speaking parts in the film, which were not great acting performances. But the film showed that Harry indeed felt comfortable in front of a movie camera.

The high point in the movie was the performances by Harry James and his Orchestra, including vocalist Helen Forrest.

Harry plays "You Made Me Love You' with an added vocal by Forrest. He also plays a choreographed version of "James Session," featuring a dance troupe of Hollywood young people.

"James Session" was a Jack Mathias composition, which paid homage to the Goodman version of "Sing, Sing, Sing." Complete with Mickey Scrima playing a Gene Krupa-like to open the tune.

The musical highlight for Harry James was the only video of him playing "Concerto for Trumpet."

While most of the music in "Private Buckaroo" was recorded on a soundstage, Harry's performance of "Concerto" seems like it was recorded live.

The complete ease with which Harry played a solo that continues to baffle trumpet players eight decades later, is astounding by any measure.

The band went back into the recording studio on June 5, 1942. Recorded during this session was "James Session," "Let Me Up," and four vocals featuring Helen Forrest.

"He's My Guy" made it to number #7 on the Billboard chart in September of 1942.

The James-Forrest pairing of "I Cried for You" debuted at #19 in September of 1942. "I Cried for You" features one of Harry's greatest ballad performances. After playing an opening solo in the key of F, the arrangement modulates to a concert A flat. Harry enters the performance on a high F. An uncommon high note for ballad records of the day.

Once again, in June of 1942, Hollywood beckoned for Harry James and His Orchestra to appear in a film.

Twentieth Century Fox began production of "Springtime in the Rockies." It was to be a Technicolor production, with a major cast slated to appear in the movie.

In addition to Harry James and His Orchestra, and Helen Forrest, Betty Grable, John Payne, Carmen Miranda, and Jackie Gleason had roles in the production.

Most of the Hollywood musicals of the 1930-40s had a musical theme, which occurred, and reoccurred throughout the film.

The "big number" in "Springtime in the Rockies" was "I Had the Craziest Dream." While the song came to be chosen by Betty Grable as her career theme song, the big hit recording was by Harry James and Helen Forrest.

The first song during the film was played with a solo by James, as he conducts his Orchestra.

Then as Helen Forrest begins her chorus, she slowly appears in a crowd, which parts as Forrest slowly advances toward the James band. Oddly, she sings with no apparent microphone. The performance was recorded on a soundstage and lip-synced by the entire James entourage.

"I Had the Craziest Dream" became forever associated with Harry James, and he recorded the song four different times. Twice with Helen Forrest, in 1942 and 1969. Also, as a trumpet solo in 1953.

Lastly, Harry recorded the "Craziest Dream" on a Japanese album featuring vocalist Kei Marimura. This was recorded in April of 1983, shortly before Harry's death. The arrangements were supposedly written by Nelson Riddle. However, Riddle had little to do with them, and they were ghostwritten for Riddle.

Harry recorded three tracks, overdubbed on tracks recorded by Japanese musicians. More about this recording session later in this book.

On September 24, 1942, Harry James and His Orchestra solidified their position as America's number one Big Band. On that night, Glenn Miller played his last radio broadcast with his stateside band. He passed the torch on the Chesterfield Radio Show, to Harry James.

Harry appeared as a walk-on surprise guest on the Chesterfield Show. He played the "Ciribiribin" portion of "Juke Box Saturday Night" with the Miller band.

By this time, everything that Harry James touched seemingly turned to gold!

Harry James and his Orchestra were unable to make any commercial records for the next two years.

On August 1, 1942, the American Federation of Musicians, led by union president James C. Petrillo, began a strike against the major American recording companies because of disagreements over royalty payments. From July 31, 1942, until November of 1944, no union musician could make a recording for any commercial record company. The 1942–44 musicians' strike remains the longest strike in entertainment history.

This was a major nail in the coffin of the Big Band Era.

Like other bands, Harry James could record V-Discs and appear on radio broadcasts, and in motion pictures. Some of the James bands' finest performances were on V-Discs.

It was during this time that James added a young viola player to his band.

Herschel Burke Gilbert was a talented musician, composer, and arranger from Milwaukee, Wisconsin. While he was still attending Julliard, he was working nights with Harry James at the Astor Hotel and the Paramount.

Although none of Gilbert's arrangements were recorded by Harry James, due to the recording band, many of his ballad arrangements were featured on radio broadcasts. He also wrote for the movies "Bathing Beauty" and "Two Girls and a Sailor."

Gilbert went on to become a prolific composer for many Hollywood movies and television shows. He wrote much of the music for "It's a Wonderful Life" and "The Rifleman."

In January of 1943, "Harry James and his Music Makers" were summoned once again to Hollywood.

(After the success of the 1941 recording of "Music Makers," which was written by Harry James, and scored by Marge Gibson, Harry began to use the term "Music Makers" as the name for his musical organization.)

"Best Foot Forward" had been a successful 1941 Broadway musical, which starred June Allyson and Nancy Walker. In 1943. MGM brought "Best Foot Forward" to the Technicolor screen.

June Allyson and Nancy Walker were joined by Lucille Ball. Harry James and His Music Makers played several numbers, including "Two O' Clock Jump."

(My dear Friend Don Boyd played the trombone solo on "Jump." He later played with Les Brown, and then settled in Columbia, South Carolina. There he became a successful and much-loved piano teacher, and played piano with many different bands in South Carolina, including my Jazz combo.)

The musical highpoint in "Best Foot Forward" was the performance of "Flight of the Bumblebee" by Harry James and His Music Makers. James played the Columbia Records version of "Bumblebee."

To watch Harry James played the difficult trumpet solo while leading the band is amazing to watch. James' flawless command of his instrument is still a marvel after nearly eight decades. The effortless execution of the tricky fingering of the solo, while in Technicolor closeups, cannot be missed.

Harry was well known for being an excellent dancer. In "Best Foot Forward," he got to demonstrate his considerable dancing skills in a musical number with Nancy Walker on "Alive and Kicking'."

December of 1943 saw the exit of Helen Forrest. Much has been written and discussed the parting of Harry and Helen.

Forrest left a huge space to fill. She was the most popular female vocalist in the country at the time.

Her immediate replacement was vocalist, Judy Williams. She was replaced within a month by Helen Ward. This being her second go-around with the James band, left no doubt that Ward was not a long-term fix for Helen Forrest's departure.

Almost immediately after the James band finished their work on "Best Foot Forward," Harry James and His Music Makers were signed to appear in a movie called "Bathing Beauty."

Red Skelton and Esther Williams were the main stars of the movie, but Harry James figured greatly in the production of the film.

Helen Forrest came in to recreate her vocal on "I Cried for You." Harry and the trumpet section performed "Trumpet Blues," which featured some interesting video tricks superimposing Harry's image in front of the band.

The most memorable musical selection in "Bathing Beauty" is Harry's performance of the celebrated violin piece "Hora Staccato." Once again, using innovative camera tricks, James is taped playing his solo live, rather than on a soundstage. Then his image is superimposed over video of the band.

While not played at the faster tempo of Rafael Mendez, or even Randy Brooks, it nonetheless demonstrated Harry's mastery of the trumpet in all genres.

Harry James and His Music Makers finished their parts in "Bathing Beauty" in enough time to begin filming their roles for the black and white movie "Two Girls and a Sailor."

Harry James and the band were involved in several musical numbers in "Two Girls and a Sailor." One significant performance was Harry and the orchestra accompanying Jimmy Durante in a comic version of Durante's signature song "Inka Dinka Doo."

Perhaps the most memorable film sequence that Harry James was ever involved with is the "Young Man with a Horn" performance with June Allyson.

It is not known who arranged the musical arrangement for "Young Man with a Horn." Jack Mathias was near the end of his relationship writing for the James band. Johnny Thompson had just recently been added to Harry's arranging team.

Strangely, there is not a lot of biographical information on Johnny Thompson. He almost certainly wrote the arrangements of "I've Heard That Song Before" and "It's Been a Long, Long Time for Harry James.

Johnny Thompson married Judy Garland's older sister Jimmie in 1948. He wrote for Tommy Dorsey, Benny Goodman, and later became a successful pop writer.

Composer-lyricist Sammy Cahn often regaled, telling the stories of the disagreements that he and Harry James had over Cahn's songs. When Sammy Cahn brought "I've Heard That Song Before," he had a ballad approach in mind.

Harry James heard it as a swing tune. Harry was right.

Then Cahn plugged a new song to James as a swing tune, "I Don't Want to Walk Without You."

James heard a ballad. James was right.

My guess is that Johnny Thompson was called upon to write the arrangement for "Young Man with a Horn" in "Two Girls and a Sailor."

Aside from a clever set of lyrics delivered by June Allyson, and a fantastic dance sequence featuring Allyson and Canadian dancer/actor Arthur Walsh, the playing of Harry James is the true focal point.

(Walsh appeared in at least forty Hollywood movies, and was one of Tinseltown's foremost exponents of the "Jitterbug" dance style.)

Harry begins the sequence with a trumpet cadenza. Then once the rhythm starts and June Allyson begins her vocal, James throws off phrase after phrase in all registers. The size and purity of tone in Harry's high range remain amazing.

Throughout most of Harry James's career, he shows the ability to PLAY in the upper register of the trumpet, rather than just hitting high notes.

There are also solos from Chuck Preble on trombone, Corky Corcoran on tenor sax, and soon to depart Claude Lakey on alto sax.

James ends the piece with a high F that he plays as effortlessly as the low notes in his solos.

In February of 1944, the Harry James Orchestra again went through some personnel changes.

Vocalist Buddy Moreno was replaced by Buddy DeVito.

Helen Ward was replaced by "Pretty" Kitty Kallen.

Kitty Kallen was the prototypical World War II "girl next door." She had a pleasant presence on the bandstand, and a voice as pretty as her face. Kallen was not the strong "belter" that Helen Forrest. But she was in the right place, at the right time, in the right band.

The biggest change, with the most lasting effect, was the replacement of Claude Lakey as lead alto sax, with Willie Smith.

Willie Smith was known as part of the "great triumvirate" of alto sax giants, along with Johnny Hodges and Benny Carter. To this day, Smith is revered by many as the greatest lead alto player of all time.

Smith had been the anchor of the Jimmie Lunceford Orchestra for ten years, both on sax and vocals. He was with the Charlie Spivak Orchestra for almost a year, before entering the Navy.

Willie Smith was as perfect for the Harry James sax section, as Corky Corcoran. He became an immediate influence on the entire James band. His powerful lead playing, and aggressive solo style had changed the sound of the Harry James Orchestra.

Harry and Willie soon became foils for each other musically.

November 21, 1944, marked the return to Columbia studios for Harry James and his Orchestra.

Kitty Kallen recorded her first side as the James band vocalist.

Duke Ellington and his alto sax star Johnny Hodges joined by lyricist Don George had written a new song. Ellington felt that "I'm Beginning to See the Light" was a sure hit. But the Duke also knew a winner when he saw one.

In 1944 Harry James was a winner!

Ellington approached James with the song. Harry James and Pee Wee Monte agreed to record the song, with the stipulation that Harry James be listed as co-composer.

Ellington reluctantly agreed, knowing that if anybody could make a hit record out of "The Light," it would be Harry James.

James handed the new song to arranger Johnny Thompson. Thompson employed an unusual voicing using Harry's trumpet, Corky's tenor, and George Davis on baritone sax on the first eight bars. Corky played a solo on the bridge. (which he repeated every night for the next thirty years!)

Then the full band came with Harry playing the last four bars of the first chorus. Allen Reuss played a four-bar solo leading into Kitty Kallen's vocal.

The arrangement closed by repeated the voicing of trumpet-tenor sax-baritone sax, modulating down to the key of D major.

When the record of "I'm Beginning to See the Light" was released in early 1945, it debuted at Number one on the Billboard charts.

Johnny Thompson's arrangement of "I'm Beginning to See the Light" for James, won the Downbeat Magazine award for the best Big Band arrangement of 1945.

A winner!

Another side recorded on November 21, 1944, was an exceptional performance of "I'm Confessin' (That I Love You). Rather than being arranged for the entire James band, it was played by a sextet.

The combo featured Harry James, Willie Smith, Arnold Ross on piano, Ed Mihelich on bass, Carl Maus on drums, and the brilliant guitarist Allen Reuss.

The number was a head arrangement made up by Harry and Willie. After Harry's exposition of the melody, Willie Smith enters with an amazing four-bar break leading into a tempo change and a Smith solo. (Listen closely, and you can hear Harry shouting encouragement to Willie Smith.)

The underrated pianist Arnold Ross plays a chorus, followed by a shout chorus by Harry, Willie, and Reuss. Allen Reuss plays a solo on the bridge, as the ensemble takes it out.

The arrangement stayed in the James book throughout the forties, fifties, and sixties. Harry James recorded "I'm Confessin'" again on MGM in 1962, retaining the flavor and zest of the original recording.

In a 1992 interview, Kitty Kallen described her time with the Harry James Orchestra.

"I sang with four bands, Jack Teagarden, Jimmy Dorsey, Harry James, and Artie Shaw. Each one had a different personality and a different approach to music. My favorite, I must tell you, was Harry James.

"He was an incredible musician. And the thing that used to astound me, he was the only musician I ever worked with that never warmed up. He would go out on bandstand cold and play like an angel.

"He also had a remarkable sense of music. He would look at a score once. He would go on air, read it once, and never, ever look at it again.

"He astounded me. You worked so hard for a man like this. I loved working for him".

The zenith for Kitty Kallen with the James band came on July 24, 1945.

Sammy Cahn had approached his partner Jule Styne with the idea of writing a song about World War II coming to an end. He wanted to have a song ready for when the boys come home.

In short measure, the songwriting team of Cahn and Styne wrote: "It's Been a Long, Long Time."

Johnny Thompson wrote the arrangement, and the James band went into the studio to record it. Kallen's "Girl next door" delivery of the verse and chorus, combined with the sound of Harry James' trumpet debuted at Number one on the Billboard charts for November 24, 1945.

Harry's opening solo was played in a romantic ballad style. However, the final chorus is performed in a "victory at last" manner, with Harry's hot trumpet riding high above the band!

No other song from the Big Band Era portrayed all the emotions of the conflict of World War II. Nearly eight decades later, it is still the single most played song when WW2 is part of a musical event.

Kitty Kallen enjoyed several additional hit records with Harry James, including "I Wish I Knew," "I'll Buy That Dream," and "11:60 P.M.".

During this time, Harry himself recorded two memorable instrumentals.

Johnny Thompson wrote the haunting and beautiful "Autumn Serenade." This recording featured one of Harry's most thrilling trumpet solos while giving Corky Corcoran and valve trombonist Juan Tizol solo exposure.

Born in Puerto Rico in 1900, Tizol was not only a pioneer as a valve trombonist but a masterful composer of Latin and other "exotic" musical genres.

Juan Tizol became a member of the Duke Ellington Orchestra in 1929. He collaborated on several famous pieces of "Ellingtonia" and is the composer of jazz standards such as "Caravan" and "Perdido."

Harry James offered Juan Tizol a job in 1944. He immediately added his composing skills to the James library, including recorded tunes "Keblah" and "Moonlight Fiesta."

Also notable as a recording forever identified with Harry James was "Carnival." Written by composers Bob Russell and Harry Warren, "Carnival" was arranged for the James band by Billy May.

When compared with the vast musical arrangements in Billy May's career, such as his work for Glenn Miller, Charlie Barnet, and the Capitol Records stable of stars, "Carnival" sounds like a "one-off" project. May felt that when it came to his music, Harry James was all business and a little bit of a taskmaster.

Billy May was also engaged to add his considerable writing skills to the next Harry James movie project.

In late 1945 Harry James and his Orchestra were engaged to appear in a movie originally titled "Kitten on the Keys," and later renamed "Do You Love Me." In this film, not only did the music of Harry James feature heavily, but Harry scored an acting role. He played a love interest, of sorts, for Maureen O'Hara. His chief rival for O'Hara's attention was none other than former James vocalist Dick Haymes.

Though neither Harry James nor Dick Haymes could ever be mistaken for serious actors, it did prove again that James was at least comfortable reciting lines in front of a camera.

The musical high point of the film was the performance of "St. Louis Blues", in which James appears to be conducting a sizeable symphonic orchestra. The number showed Harry James playing the trumpet in several different styles, all in one tune. As always, Harry's masterful technique in "St. Louis Blues", stands as one of the best-recorded examples of who Harry James was musically.

Changes

The unintended victims of the Musicians Union recording ban of 1943-44, were the musicians themselves. Not only did the ban proves that people would buy records WITHOUT musicians appearing on the records, buy the fickleness of the people who buy records, shifted their allegiances to the singers.

Vocalists such as Frank Sinatra, Dick Haymes, Perry Como, Jo Stafford all had hit records backed only by choral groups singing acapella.

Although Harry James had several records hit the Billboard charts during this period, they were all records that had not been huge hits and were reissued by Columbia Records. "Cherry," "I'll Get

By," and "All or Nothing at All" were snatched up by Harry James fans desperate for his recordings.

Another result of the recording ban was that the focus of the Big Bands, was no longer the leader of the band, but the vocalists of those bands.

Big Bands like Woody Herman, Benny Goodman, and Tommy Dorsey, disbanded in late 1946.

Although Marion Morgan and Buddy DeVito were credible singers, they were not the drawing card for the Harry James Orchestra.

Harry James was also forced to disband and retool for the ever-changing music industry.

At the height of the James band's success, Harry employed as many as twenty-seven music musicians. By the end of 1947, the Harry James Orchestra consisted of seventeen musicians.

Harry began only using the strings for recording sessions.

One of these sessions, from February 10, 1947, featured a once in a lifetime trumpet section consisting of Paul Geil, Mannie Klein, Uan Rasey, and Zeke Zarchy.

James also added two new arrangers to the writing team. In addition to Jack Mathias and Johnny Thompson, Neal Hefti and Ray Conniff joined the band. Hefti briefly joined the trumpet section, but he was brought in to rekindle the Jazz flame in the James crew.

Neal Hefti had been a part of Woody Herman's band, where he played trumpet and wrote such Woodchopper classics as "The Good Earth," "Wildroot," and "Blowin' Up a Storm." He was also writing for Count Basie.

Harry James was very informed about the influence of "Bebop" upon Big Band music, and Jazz music in general. Dizzy Gillespie, and later Miles Davis were close friends with Harry.

Harry most admired the total abandon with the new generation of jazz soloists. He also was impressed by the technical styles that players like Dizzy, Fats Navarro, and Miles used.

The player that Harry James most admired from the 1950s and after that was Clifford Brown.

My Friend Chuck Anderson, who was the trombone soloist for the James band in the 1970-80s, once told me a story about Clifford Brown.

He said that one night, while the band was traveling by bus, he heard music coming from the front of the bus. There was Harry James, sitting in his customary seat. He was listening to a cassette tape of Clifford Brown.

Chuck said that Harry had tears streaming down his face. He asked, "Why did God take Clifford Brown and leave me?"

Brown's influence on the ballad playing of Harry James, in particular, is apparent in several recordings from the late 1950s and early 1960s. Including "Lover Man" and "Willow Weep for Me."

Harry James approached arranger Neal Hefti about writing some "Bop flavored" charts for the band. Hefti began offering charts like The Arrival", "There They Go" and "Rank Frank."

Listening to those early Neal Hefti compositions for James showed just how great the Harry James Orchestra was. For most of Harry's career, his bands took a back seat to no other band!

The James-Hefti relationship continued throughout the next fifteen years.

Ray Conniff had even more of an effect on the James band. He began writing for Harry in 1945, and for the next decade, Ray Conniff was Harry's primary arranger.

Not only did Ray Conniff write excellent Swing compositions like "The Beaumont Ride" and "The Last Mile', but he was a master at writing arrangements of pop-oriented songs.

A large percentage of the James library from 1947-1954, had Ray Conniff's signature on the arrangement. Those included "September Song," "Vine Street Blues," and "Tango Blues."

From the first chart that Conniff wrote for Harry James in 1945, "Easy" to the last one, Conniff wrote in 1954, "Charmaine," Ray Conniff wrote 222 arrangements for Harry James and his Orchestra.

According to a 1998 interview, Ray Conniff told it this way:

"I had been writing for the Harry James band...Harry and I had a parting of the ways, a few years down the road. I was doing an awful lot of writing, a lot of originals for him. He had a song he wanted me to write. I remember the song was "Ruby.""

"Harry said 'Why don't you write a little bit of a "Bop" treatment on this?'"

"Bop was kind of a new school of music coming along, and I never did dig Bop...It was not my bag. So, I said, 'You know Harry, I just don't feel that kind of music. Maybe it's time you got another boy.' And his jaw dropped. He looked at me like he couldn't believe what I was saying."

"So Harry said, 'OK," and I left the band."

Harry once explained in an interview, how he viewed the divergent styles among Jazz musicians and Big Bands:

"I think there's room in our profession for a wide variety of styles, and I can't see any reason for knocking any artist or any style, just because it doesn't happen to be your own. What we need in music is more students and fewer people knocking what they don't like or can't understand."

"Too many musicians in recent years have played as if they were trying to run before they can walk. The foundation, background, and schooling are indispensable. Otherwise, what comes out of your horn is just a jumble. It's essential to become a musician first and foremost, not an exhibitionist."

"We're happy to have a library that represents so many phases of music."

Harry James was trying to add the newer "Bebop" styles of playing and writing into his musical persona during the late 1940s. There are significant examples of Harry appropriating these styles into his own Jazz solos.

Listen, for example, to the Neal Hefti composition "Proclamation." After solos by clarinetist Eddie Rosa, Corky Corcoran, and Willie Smith, there is a sizable back and forth between Harry James and the entire band.

During 1947-48, Harry appeared in two more Hollywood musicals. "If I'm Lucky" was a routine treatment of the "Boy meets Girl" plot, with Perry Como and Vivian Blaine. Neither the movie nor the music was memorable. Although with Harry having a speaking part, he proved he had better acting skills than Perry Como.

"Carnegie Hall" was a typical Hollywood musical using the famed concert venue as the center of the period piece. Harry James plays "All the World is Mine" in a symphonic setting.

During this period, Harry James recorded several sides in a combo setting. "You'll Never Know" featured a "jazzier" treatment of the Oscar-winning ballad. Harry and Corky are featured.

"Pagan Love Song" gives a slight nod to "Bebop" and features Carl "Ziggy" Elmer on trombone, Eddie Rosa on clarinet, and sounding more like Artie Shaw than Artie Shaw. Willie Smith and Harry lead the fast-paced arrangement.

"Cottontail" is delivered by an octet, in which James shows off his technique, and gives a fiery solo by Willie Smith. Elmer plays a short solo, which leads the entire combo into a reading of Duke Ellington's sax ensemble passage of his own composition.

It is more than evident that James possessed more than enough technique and knowledge of even the most complex chord structure, to play even the most difficult passages.

However, he couldn't stop being Harry James. His ventures into the world of "Bebop" are never convincing enough to show that he could ever be comfortable in that realm.

Composer, arranger, and saxophonist Jimmy Mundy established his reputation as a master of writing "Swing" arrangements in the early thirties. His writing for Benny Goodman remains among the best examples in the "Swing" genre. He was the arranger of the immortal "Sing, Sing, Sing" for the 1937 Goodman band.

At the same time that Harry James was dipping his musical toes into the "Bop" waters, he was still adding "Swing" charts to his sizable library.

Harry commissioned Jimmy Mundy to write some fresh new charts for his string-less band. Mundy added tunes like "Snooty Frooty" and "Poppin' Off," both of which were recorded by James.

The most important contribution by Jimmy Mundy was his 1948 composition "Ultra."

"Ultra" was written using the chord structure of "How High the Moon." In fact, the melody of "Ultra" almost sounds like it could be used as a countermelody to "How High the Moon."

"How High the Moon" had been in the James library as early as 1940. The tune was first used as a vocal feature for Dick Haymes. It also appeared as a feature for the brilliant pianist Arnold Ross in 1946.

The "Bebop" culture had adopted "How High the Moon" as an anthem. Numerous "Bebop" musicians had composed tunes built on the chord changes for "Moon."

Jimmy Mundy took the difficult chord structure and inserted it into a hard-swinging arrangement for the Harry James Orchestra. After the initial brassy blast of the opening bars, the melody is delivered first by an unlikely voice in a trumpet player's Big Band, a baritone sax.

Bob Poland served as the baritone sax player for James for over a decade. He switched to tenor sax in the late fifties when multi-instrumentalist Ernie Small took over the baritone chair.

Poland had a warm sound on baritone, in contrast with the average baritone sax players of the day, who tended to have a rougher edge to their tone.

After Bob Poland delivers the melody on baritone sax, the band begins a chorus of "back and forth" with Harry James.

After seventy years, the James solo on "Ultra" remains staggering in its execution. I have looked at a transcription of Harry's solo and still try to figure out how he did it. He runs through every register of his horn while he manages to touch all the intricate chord changes.

Within a short period, Harry's solo on "Ultra" developed into a pattern solo, from which he rarely deviated.

To this day, I have never heard another trumpet player, including myself, successfully replicate the complicated solo.

Very soon after the commercial recording was released in July of 1949, James had Mundy rewrite the chart to include Willie Smith replacing Harry's back and forth with the band. Mundy also added a complete chorus by Corky Corcoran on tenor sax.

I have heard many different performances of "Ultra," including seeing him play it live. He invariably shouted, "GO!" at the trombone section slide in the last chorus.

Among diehard Harry James fans, "Ultra" remains THE best example of Harry's mastery and the power of the Harry James Orchestra!

Coasting

As the 1950s unfolded, Harry James entered a new phase as a celebrity and Big Band Leader.

Harry James and Betty Grable, seemed to be living a comfortable life on their sixty-two acre "Baby-J Ranch in Calabasas, California.

Harry and Betty share a relaxed evening at Ben Pollack's restaurant with Harry's dad, who was also a musician.

The Harry James Orchestra still toured, but less often. Harry continued to appear on television shows, usually based in Los Angeles. He appeared in the 1950 movie musical "I'll Get By." It was a bad movie with an incomprehensible plot. The timelines in the film made no sense.

It did give Harry a chance to play two excellent ballad performances, "I'll Get By" and "Once in a While."

The new long-playing record allowed the James band to record a series of "Danceable" albums. They were largely dance band versions of the pop tunes of the day.

Ray Conniff got the lion's share of the arranging duties. And Harry James played some of the best ballad solos of his career.

A recording session from June 9, 1950, allows Harry to record another memorable performance.

Percy Faith composed "Brazilian Sleigh Bells" in 1950. He also recorded it for a Columbia Records album called "Dance Date with Percy Faith."

Harry James heard the song and felt like it would be a fit for his trumpet player skills, and as a feature for his trumpet section. James recorded it during the June 1950 session for his album "Dance Date with Harry James."

"Brazilian Sleigh Bells" was not released on the "Dance Date" album, but as a single.

The James band did perform the tune on a 1958 TV show "The Big Record" with Patti Page.

The recording remains in the canon of great Harry James performances.

No one seemed to know why author Dorothy Baker wrote: "Young Man with a Horn" in 1938. It has been described as having been loosely based on the tragic life of cornetist Bix Beiderbecke.

However, even the most casual research into Beiderbecke's life yields very little resemblance between Bix and the protagonist of Baker's book, Rick Martin, aside from alcohol abuse.

The book was a sad portrayal of a Jazz musician, who couldn't find his own value or the value in any other person. He stubbornly clung to his trumpet and a bottle, until the tragic end.

The book struck a chord with Hollywood director Michael Curtiz.

Curtiz had been a long-time successful director starting with silent movies. He was taken by the "Rick Martin" character in the book. "Martin" seemed to be unable to make a correct choice in life, especially in his relationships.

The undercurrent of a "lesbian" character likely presented Michael Curtiz with a challenge, of how he could show the theme in a less than overt way—still getting his point across.

Unlike the sad ending in the book, Curtiz felt that he could never devote an entire movie to a man's life, and then kill him off at the end. Curtiz opted for a "Hollywood ending."

Several years before producing "Young Man with a Horn," Michael Curtiz already knew who would characterize the lead character in the film.

He wanted John Garfield to play "Rick Martin," and bandleader/trumpet player Harry James would supply the musical voice.

John Garfield would have been the perfect choice to play Martin. He was not a method actor, like Kirk Douglas, and would truly have given a real core to the mixed-up trumpet player of the movie.

"The Red Scare" erupted in Hollywood in the late 1940s, and John Garfield got sucked into the controversy. John Garfield was eventually blacklisted in Hollywood, and his film acting career was essentially over.

Kirk Douglas had just recently gained notoriety with his Oscar nomination for the 1949 movie "Champion." Michael offered Douglas the "Rick Martin" part in "Young Man with a Horn," and he accepted.

I will not attempt to critique the film, as I am not a professional movie critic. Suffice to say, the music of Harry James and Doris Day are the highlights of the film. The movie was not a huge success, making the absence of John Garfield all the more disappointing.

Harry James playing the trumpet solos for Kirk Douglas, and was, unsuccessfully, given the responsibility of trying to teach Kirk Douglas how to look like a trumpet player.

James was unsuccessful in his task, though it was not Harry's fault. Kirk Douglas was not an apt student.

Trumpeter Jimmy Zito was hired to fill the horn for the "Art Hazard" character. Zito was a big Harry James fan, and there are parts of the film where it is nearly impossible to tell the difference between Harry James and Jimmy Zito.

(Harry once said to me that Warner Brothers had him go back and replace some of Zito's performances in the soundtrack, with his own. However, I have no way to verify that.)

The magnificent sound of Harry James was never presented more successfully than in "Young Man with a Horn." The playing on "With a Song in My Heart" alone stands as one of Harry's best performances.

The commercially released album of "Young Man with a Horn" was recorded on January 25-27, 1950. Two more tracks were recorded on January 5, 1951.

Doris Day and Harry James recorded in the studio, as overdubbing was not quite perfected by Columbia at that time.

The Doris Day/Harry James album was the last real success that Harry James had at Columbia Records. IN 1950, Mitch Miller left Mercury Records, where he had been commercially successful, and became the A&R director at Columbia. It became clear that Mitch Miller was not concerned at all with Jazz records.

He began making all the decisions about which songs would be assigned to which musical artist.

Miller leaned toward commercial, gimmicky songs. Something that Harry James had never done. Mitch Miller began pairing new, less well-known singers, with musicians who had been successful at selling records.

Harry James had sold a lot of records for Columbia. No other big band had sold as many records up to 1950 as Harry James and his Orchestra.

James soon found himself on record dates with Toni Harper, Jerry Vale, in addition to former James singers Kitty Kallen and Frank Sinatra.

The only record that was commercially successful was the May 1952 sessions for "Hollywood's Best" with Rosemary Clooney.

The arrangements that Ray Conniff wrote for the "Hollywood's Best" album were lush, and some were almost breathtaking, as Clooney and James followed each other in and out of the Academy Award-winning songs.

The album hit number three on the Billboard Pop Album charts, and "You'll Never Know" was in the top ten for a week. To this day, "You'll Never Know" remains among the most endearing records of Harry James' career.

Much has been written about the highly publicized "Great James Robbery" from April of 1951.

Duke Ellington had truly built the "sound" of his Big Band around the luscious sound of Johnny Hodges' alto sax. If any musician could ever be truly indispensable, Hodges was.

In April 1951, Johnny Hodges left the Duke Ellington Orchestra to start his own combo. The void he left in the Ellington band, was unexpected.

Ellington approached drummer Louis Bellson, who was playing drums for Harry James, if he would like to join his band, and bring Willie Smith and Juan Tizol with him.

Duke Ellington described it himself in 1951:

"There is no such thing as a "replacement" in my band. A new musician means for us a new sound and the creation of new music, which he, and he alone, can properly express."

In truth, the Ellington band didn't skip a beat. Willie Smith brought new energy to the Ellington sax section, and the Bellson presence was monumental.

Harry James was not easily discouraged. In fact, he teasingly told the three departing musicians to see if Ellington needed a trumpet player!

By 1951, Jazz was not the driving motivation for Harry James. His commercial success had been cemented years before. He was still a "household name," especially due to his continued marriage to Betty Grable.

Jackie Mills returned to the drum chair. Mascagni "Musky" Ruffo joined the band as the lead alto.

Dave Robbins became the lead trombonist and would fill that position several times for the next two decades. Robbins was a brilliant musician and arranger.

In late 1951, Ray Conniff suggested to Harry that he would like to write updated versions of some of the tunes that Harry James had been featured on with the Benny Goodman Orchestra.

Conniff wrote arrangements of "Roll 'Em," "Down South Camp Meeting," "Stealin' Apples." And "Don't Be That Way."

The James band recorded "Don't Be That Way" and "Roll 'Em" for Columbia. Conniff had replaced Goodman's clarinet with Harry's trumpet. He also rewrote some of the voicings for the sax section in particular. For "Don't Be That Way," Ray Conniff took the original Harry James solo from the 1937 RCA record with Goodman and wrote it out for the trumpet section.

Harry James used "Don't Be That Way" for the opening tune for the rest of his career. Because it had given the young James his first solo at the famed 1938 Carnegie Hall concert, Harry considered the song as his good luck charm.

"Don't Be That Way" was one of forty-six tunes played on a television show starring Harry James and his Orchestra.

"The Harry James Show" debuted on January 12, 1952. Filmed in Hollywood, the first episode was in a game show format. Everyone concerned quickly realized that if you were going to feature a World-Famous bandleader on a weekly show, it should feature his music.

From the second show on, "The Harry James Show" became a variety show. Several guests appeared on the show, including Harry's former boss Ben Pollack. Harry also featured himself on drums during a couple of episodes.

The show only lasted one season. However, it did serve to keep Harry James in the public eye.

In September of 1952, Corky Corcoran once again left the James band to form a small group in his hometown of Tacoma, Washington. It was two years before he returned to the James fold.

In Corcoran's absence, Francis "Polly" Polifrani became Harry's go-to tenor soloist, although Bill Massingill, Herb Steward, and Herb Lorden occasionally played some tenor sax solos.

October of 1952 found the Harry James Orchestra appearing at the famed Aragon Ballroom in Chicago. During the extended stand at the Aragon, Columbia Records decided to record a "Live" album of the James band.

The album was called "One Night Stand" and was largely a Jazz oriented album.

Some of the tunes on the album included Neal Hefti's chart on "You Go To My Head," which is one of Harry's all-time finest ballad performances. Also, on the album was a Neal Hefti tune called "There They Go," which had been in the James book since 1948.

A comparatively laid-back treatment of "Ultra" had solos by Herb Steward on alto and "Polly" Polifrani on tenor sax.

One of the strangest choices that Harry James ever made was adding accordion player Tommy Gumina to the band. Gumina was a great accordion virtuoso. However, in my opinion, he did not add anything to the Harry James band.

Gumina was featured on the Columbia single of "Ruby." On the "One Night Stand" album, Gumina and James played an interesting version of "Flight of the Bumblebee." It forced Harry to play "Bumblebee" in the key of "A" concert, to accommodate

Gumina's accordion, being a C instrument. (Harry's total mastery of the trumpet allowed him to play a brief harmony to Gumina's melody in the second half of the performance!)

Bernard (Round One)

When Harry James first met Bernard "Buddy" Rich, James saw in Rich a kindred spirit of sorts. Their childhoods and upbringing couldn't be more similar.

Harry grew up with his parents touring with the circus. Buddy grew up with his parents touring in Vaudeville.

To be honest, neither man had a childhood. They were performing as toddlers. That fact caused both Harry James and Buddy Rich to have certain insecurities as adults. Both were, to an extent, perpetual teenagers. They were hardly equipped to deal with success or relationships.

Harry James knew that Buddy Rich was going to be a giant as Jazz drummer when he saw him in 1938 at the St. Regis jam sessions with Joe Marsala's band.

When Buddy Rich turned down Harry's offer to join his fledging Big Band in 1939, a kind of obsession began to grow in Harry's mind. He was never going to be happy until Buddy Rich was his drummer.

Rich again rejected James' offer to join his band when Rich came home from the Marines in 1945. Rich felt the time was right to venture out with his own Big Band. Aided with money from his old nemesis Frank Sinatra, Rich formed a Big Band in 1946. However, Buddy's resistance to pandering to dancers led to the short run as a leader.

Still, Harry James wouldn't give up!

March 1953 found Harry James and His Music Makers with a two-week extended stand at the "Band Box" night club in New York City. The "Band Box" was a Broadway night club, that was directly next door to "Birdland."

Harry particularly enjoyed playing Jazz clubs. Even into the 1970s, Harry felt a sense of accomplishment at entertaining hardcore Jazz aficionados.

The opening act for the James band at the "Band Box" was a four-piece combo led by Buddy Rich. The combo included Hank Jones on piano, Curly Russell on bass, and mellophone and vibes player Don Elliott.

During the two-week engagement, James would drop in and listen to Buddy's group. On several occasions, Harry sat in with the Rich combo.

Harry also extended an offer for Buddy Rich to sit in with the James band, which Rich did.

It only served to intensify Harry's obsession to get Buddy Rich in his band.

When the "Band Box" stand was completed, Harry again offered Buddy Rich a job.

This time, the circumstances were different. James was a successful bandleader. He had already begun to hold court at Nevada hotel-casinos. The tours by the Harry James Orchestra were shorter and less frequent. That meant that Buddy Rich could continue to freelance when the James band was dormant.

James offered Rich a contract worth about $35,000 a year. An astronomical sum for a drummer.

There was a problem, almost from the beginning with the James-Rich partnership. According to Rich, part of the deal that the two men had struck, was that Buddy Rich would get feature billing on all advertising and the bandstand.

It became apparent from day one that Harry James wasn't going to change his style. He still relied on dancers for the bulk of his performing income. So, the tempos he set, remained perfect for dancing, with plenty of ballads.

James did give Buddy his drum features, and the occasional vocal (with Harry James playing drums).

Sam Donahue wrote a tune that would feature Buddy called the "Palladium Party." The James band recorded the "Palladium Party" on April 6, 1953.

It soon began wearing on Buddy's ego. Every time the Harry James Orchestra went into a recording studio, it was to wax ballad features for Harry's horn.

One album that was a definite departure for Harry and Buddy was a "Live" recording from the Hollywood Palladium during a two-week stand from December and January.

Buddy's drums were featured on "Sugar Foot Stomp" and "Flash." "Flash" featured an amazing back and forth between Buddy and his Boss.

Rich also sang "Ain't She Sweet" accompanied by Harry James on the drums. (Listen closely to the laughter at Harry's drum breaks!"

"Dancing in Person with Harry James At the Hollywood Palladium" is probably the most enduring recording from the 1950s Columbia years for Harry James.

The next recording session in 1954 was ballads, ballads, and more ballads.

Buddy didn't feel like he was given enough respect and notoriety in the James rhythm section. Also, everything that the Harry James Orchestra played was played for dancers.

By July of 1954, Buddy Rich had had enough. He abruptly left the James band and was replaced by Louis Bellson.

December 1954 saw the James band back in the studio to record several tracks. Some of the tracks were for an upcoming album, which would not be completed until February of 1955.

Arrangements by Neal Hefti, Shorty Rogers, and Louis Bellson were recorded. Half of the album "Jazz Session" included Louis Bellson on drums and Larry Kinnamon on piano. The February session had Gene Estes on drums, and famed harpist Corky Hale is replacing Kinnamon on piano.

By no means had Harry James "gotten over" Buddy Rich!

Capitol and Basie

William James "Count" Basie led a band for almost fifty years. Although he pared down to an octet briefly in 1949-50, he came roaring back with a new Big Band in 1952.

The Big Band that Basie led during the 1950s and early 1960s has often been called his "New Testament" band. It relied more on arrangers and ensemble precision. Though there were solid soloists, it was the sound that remained consistent and recognizable.

Basie built his Big Band using a library that was, in large part, written by Neal Hefti and Ernie Wilkins.

Hefti had already been writing for Harry James since 1947.

Ernie Wilkins had been free-lancing all over the Jazz landscape since 1951 and was writing for Basie and the Dorsey Brothers. Wilkins was a brilliant writer, who excelled at writing for the character and sound of the Big Band he was writing for at the time.

From the beginning of his bandleading career, Harry James respected, and at times tried to emulate the Basie sound. As far back as 1940, James played tunes that were associated with the Count Basie Orchestra, including "Shorty George," "9:20 Special." And "Moten Swing."

In 1955, the Count Basie Orchestra had been sharing the marquee at Birdland with Jazz organist Wild Bill Davis. Davis had become known for his distinctive version of "April in Paris." He recorded "April in Paris" on a live album at Birdland.

(One interesting fact is that the drummer for Wild Bill Davis at Birdland was Chris Columbus. Columbus was the father of drummer Sonny Payne, who was the drummer for Count Basie, and eventually for the Harry James Orchestra.)

The story goes that Basie asked Davis to write an arrangement for the Basie band, and that would be recorded on an album with Wild Bill Davis as guest with the Basie band.

Supposedly, Davis had to cancel the record date. So, the Count Basie Orchestra recorded it without Davis.

The Basie recording of "April in Paris" got a lot of radio play and helped to sell a lot of records.

Harry James took notice immediately!

He approached Ernie Wilkins with the idea of writing a version of "April in Paris" for the Harry James Orchestra.

Capitol Records had become a major record label in the decade after the Big Band Era had ended. Thanks in large part to Frank Sinatra, Capitol was a player with the record-buying public.

Capitol decided to launch a series of records featuring some of the biggest names in Big Band music.

The Capitol Records studios were world-renown for the technical innovations that Capitol had implemented. Pioneers in sound-insulation technology, Capitol studios provided a superior method for recording a Big Band.

The Big Bands of Ray Anthony, Duke Ellington, Les Brown, Woody Herman, Glen Gray, Benny Goodman, and Stan Kenton, all were signed by Capitol Records for a "Big Bands in Hi-Fi" series of albums.

Benny Goodman was basking in the renewed interest in his music, that had come from the motion picture "The Benny Goodman Story."

Harry James had appeared in a sequence of the film, where he recreated his solos on "Shine" and "Sing, Sing, Sing." Because Harry had been hugging the West Coast and reduced his touring for much of the 1950s, many moviegoers were surprised to see that Harry James was playing better than ever.

All these combined factors made Harry James and his Orchestra a natural fit for Capitol Records.

During a week of recording sessions in mid-July of 1955, Harry James and his Orchestra recorded the tracks for the album "Harry James in Hi-Fi." James added Conrad Gozzo to the trumpet section for the recordings.

Conrad Gozzo, to this day, is known as perhaps the greatest lead trumpet player of all time. He had been playing for Harry James at the band's home stands at the Hollywood Palladium for much of early 1955.

James brought in Helen Forrest to recreate hers and Kitty Kallen's vocal hits with the James band. Vocalist Bob Marlo sang Dick Haymes's vocal on "My Silent Love."

Harry's trumpet had never been so well recorded, and the fresh new recordings of the James hits from the 1940s, caused the album "Harry James in Hi-Fi" to debut in the Billboard top ten list for Best Selling records in November 1955.

Capitol wasted no time rounding up the James organization for "More Harry James in H-Fi' in November of 1955.

Harry used three different drummers for the Capitol sessions. Jackie Mills, Buddy Combine, and Gene Estes all took part in the recordings.

Famed session drummer Gene Estes provided the" Gene Krupa-like" solos on "James Session," finishing out the track with just Estes and James to close.

Arranger Ernie Wilkins supplied two charts for the Capitol sessions. An original "Walkin' Home," and the James version of "April in Paris."

The tracks were not released on the Harry James albums but were included in a Capitol sampler album called "Dance to the Bands," which was released in early 1956.

To a casual listener, the James record of "April in Paris" might have sounded like a copy of sorts, of the Basie version. But the differences between the Basie and James recordings are stark.

Harry's "April in Paris" is more of a Jazz-tinged treatment than the Count Basie record. The presence of Willie Smith on lead alto, and soloing, give an edge to Harry.

The "One More Time" quotes from Basie himself, were replaced by Joe Comfort on walking bass.

Finally, the fact that Conrad Gozzo was leading the trumpet section, and Harry James soloing in all registers, and at the top of his game, make the Harry James recording of "April in Paris" the superior rendering.

Also not released by Capitol, were recordings of "Hora Staccato" and "Ultra." It is not known why they were not released, other than Harry being dissatisfied with the results.

While Harry was finishing up the November Capitol sessions, he was invited to take part in a Benny Goodman recording session.

The soundtrack to "The Benny Goodman Story" was released on Decca Records. However, Goodman was under contract to Capitol, and they wanted a piece of the BG Story.

Benny assembled a truly "All-Star" band for the album "Mr. Benny Goodman."

The Benny Goodman Orchestra for the Capitol dates included:

HARRY JAMES, RUDY BRAFF, DOC SEVERINSEN,

CHRIS GRIFFIN, BILLY BUTTERFIELD, BERNIE PREVIN (tp),

URBIE GREEN, WILL BRADLEY (TB)

PHIL BODNER (as); AL KLINK, PEANUTS HUCKO (ts); DICK HYMAN (p)

TONY MOTTOLA (g); MILT HINTON, GEORGE DUVIVIER (b) BOBBY DONALDSON (d).

Harry James soloed on "Shine," and "One O'Clock Jump." Harry also recreated his iconic solo on "Sing, Sing, Sing," by starting his solo an octave higher than the original.

Harry was also called upon to recreate Ziggy Elman's solo on "And the Angels Sing."

(Elman's health issued had forced him to quit playing the trumpet.)

The year 1956 saw Harry James resume his quest to tap into the "Basie Sound."

Ernie Wilkins was joined by other arrangers, including Les Brown veteran arranger J. Hill, Bill Holman, and James band veterans Larry Kinnamon and Herb Lorden.

Harry began to amass a very Basie-like library. A study of the Harry James Orchestra from the time revealed that Harry played very few of his own "hits." The sets were filled with originals and jazzy versions of standards.

(Harry's refusal to play his 1940s hits, was a never-ending source of conflict between Harry and his longtime manager Frank "Pee Wee" Monte." Those conflicts continued until Harry died in 1983. When Monte reformed the Harry James "ghost band" in 1984, he hired Jack Mathias to rewrite the "hits" without the string parts.)

Other than appearing in a Universal music short called "Riot in Rhythm," Harry took the first few weeks of 1956 off.

Bernard (Round Two)

During the "retirement" phase for Harry James, which ran from 1954-1957, Harry tried fronting an octet. There are two entire albums from 1954, featuring vocalist Peggy King, and the Harry James Jazz Octet.

There were personnel changes during the appearances of the HJ Octet.

It consisted of Nick Buono on trumpet, Herb Steward or Corky Corcoran on tenor, Willie Smith on alto, Herb Lorden on tenor and clarinet, Juan Tizol on trombone, and a rhythm section with Larry Kinnamon on piano, Floyd Blanton on bass, and Buddy Rich on drums.

Buddy Rich also got to sing occasionally, with Harry on drums.

Also, during this period, Harry James appeared in another Hollywood movie. "The Opposite Sex" was an updated version of the Hollywood classic "The Women," only without the fine acting.

The director of this horrible movie developed a "Dream" sequence, in which June Allyson's character, daydreamed of the famous sequence from "Two Girls and a Sailor." However, instead of recreating the music from the former picture, Harry James appeared with a small version of his band, with James dressed in military clothing at a USO show.

Harry and June Allyson "lip-synced" to the soundtrack from the 1944 film.

It was a bizarre scene from a bad movie!

In April of 1956, Harry James and his Octet made an appearance on "The Milton Berle Show."

Harry had called Buddy Rich and asked him to make the "Berle" show, which was televised from the U.S.S Hancock, which was a Naval aircraft carrier. The logistics of performing on the deck of an aircraft carrier, with its wind-current effects, was made even more uncomfortable for Harry, Buddy and the boys.

They appeared on the same program with Elvis Presley!

The surviving kinescope of the "Milton Berle" program shows just how difficult the performance was for the James group.

The television gig led to Buddy Rich moving in and out of the James Band for the next year.

Appearances with Harry James at the Hollywood Palladium allowed Rich to continue to record with studio groups of his own.

One radio broadcast from June 9, 1956, showed Harry and Buddy in fine fettle.

In addition to the James versions of "Stealin' Apples," "Ultra," and "Bee Gee," Buddy sings a song from his Verve album "Buddy Rich Sings Johnny Mercer." ("How about Harry James on drums? Said the radio announcer!)

January of 1957 gave Harry James opportunities to appear with Les Brown's band on "The Bob Hope Chevy Show." Harry played an abridged version of "The Brave Bulls."

Harry also guested and accompanied his wife, Betty Grable, at the Academy Awards ceremony in April 1957.

Here is a good place to discuss an aspect of Harry James' trumpet playing that was well demonstrated during the "retirement" period.

To be sure, Harry James never truly retired. He continued to perform until nine days before his death on July 5, 1983.

He did scale back his public performances from 1954 to early 1957. He had made a conscious decision to enjoy his celebrity status, and to tour significantly less.

He and Betty were committed to raising and racing horses. He spent more time at "Barn 12" at Delmar than in front of his band.

During this time, Harry took weeks and even months without touching a trumpet.

I have been playing the trumpet for over fifty-one years, as of this writing. I HAVE to play regularly if I want to maintain a semblance of good technique and stamina.

Harry James was not like most of the rest of us trumpet players. He could go weeks without playing, and then walk on to a stage and play like Harry James.

As I have written in this book, Harry believed trumpet playing was all about breath support. And of course, to an extent, that is true.

Others, like Jerome Callet and his devotees, have said that Harry had this "special embouchure," which enabled him to play without daily maintenance.

There is no doubt that Harry James had the "perfect" embouchure. His chops were the strongest and most consistent I have ever seen. And I have seen several of the greats up close.

Harry James was different. He had an indefinable quality that separated him from the legions of trumpet players, before and after him.

His chops withstood decades of chain-smoking and alcohol abuse. Those abuses began to cause the deterioration of his teeth when he was in his forties. From 1964 on, he had to deal with dental implants, which were very primitive when compared with today's implant technology.

His teeth and the resultant implants caused him severe pain off and on for nearly twenty years, until his death.

My friend Tony Scodwell has told me stories of Harry being in so much pain, that he relied on Tony to play ensemble parts that were reserved for Harry.

Tony once explained it this way:

"I then rejoined Harry James' Big Band on lead in 1968. A fine recording called "The Golden Trumpet of Harry James" was done in Hollywood with Tutti Camarata producing. Tutti wanted to recreate Harry's biggest hits with London Phase 4 technology. If you've heard this recording, notice that the lead is missing on the out chorus of A-Train. Harry had all of his lower teeth replaced with implants four days before the recording. We had done the first take of A-Train without a problem, but Harry felt he might get a better solo with one more take and, wanting to rest, didn't play the lead in the section the second time. Guess what take Tutti chose? I'm not sure why, but it may have something to do with the start of this three-hour session. Tutti said to Harry to tune up the band, and Harry said: "This band plays, it doesn't tune-up!" It's a good recording and is still available."

And yet, he always recovered and returned to the top, or near top form.

Harry didn't practice like the rest of the brass playing world. He didn't warm up.

When he was struggling with his "new" dentures in the mid-1960s, he would sometime play some exercises from "Clarke's Technical Studies." Not to strengthen his chops, but to see and feel where his chops were limited.

His "warmup" sometimes consisted of a four-octave chromatic run, from low G to double-high G.

Then he walked onto the stage and started "Ciribiribin" and "Don't Be That Way."

Capitol Records asked Harry to prepare to record a new album in early 1957.

Harry was more excited about the next Capitol project than perhaps anything he had ever recorded.

The band had been playing several originals by Ernie Wilkins, Bill Holman, and J. Hill, for nearly two years. The sets from the

Hollywood Palladium dates from 1955-57 were filled with Jazz charts.

So, when Harry booked the recording dates for the Capitol Tower, he knew what he was going to play.

He also knew who would be in the band. Willie Smith was indispensable on lead alto. His powerful sound was as recognizable as Harry's trumpet.

Corky Corcoran was back in Tacoma, performing and recording under his name. But Harry felt in his core that this new record was going to be pivotal in establishing, at least in his mind, the Harry James Big Band as a Jazz organization.

Harry asked Corky to play on the record, and Corcoran returned to the band for the remaining months of 1957.

As in the case of several brass players in Harry's bands over the years, young Don Paladino was recommended by Stan Kenton as a fine lead trumpet player. Paladino had started with Les Brown in the early 1950s, before joining Kenton's band.

Along with Don Paladino, veteran trumpet player Bob Rolfe left Kenton's band to join Harry.

Longtime trumpet player Art Depew was brought in for four of the tracks on the Capitol album, as was Ray Linn on six tracks.

Then there was the ever-present Nick "The Count" Buono.

Trombonist Herbie Harper was firmly ensconced in the "West Coast Jazz" scene. He came in to lead the James trombone section for four tracks.

Zoot Sims' older brother Ray Sims had been in Les Brown's band for almost a decade before he became part of the Capitol Records stable of top-notch players. Sims came on to play trombone on six tracks on the new James album and stayed for the next twenty years.

Ray Sims was an emotional ballad player, and his work was greatly reminiscent of the trombone playing of Bill Harris. He was also by most accounts, a steadying factor with his relatively calm demeanor.

Herb Lorden was a brilliant sax player, and clarinetist. He was also a gifted arranger. He was one of the best clarinetists of the Artie Shaw school of clarinet playing. Herb Lorden arranged and performed Artie Shaw's "Concerto for Clarinet" for the 1954 James album "Jazz Session."

Legendary guitarist Allen Reuss and Harry James worked together in Benny Goodman's band. He also spent several years in Harry's band during the mid-1940s.

Reuss was a perfect voice for the new James rhythm section. Larry Kinnamon had been playing piano for several years, Harry James, since 1954 and was also a fine arranger.

James knew he HAD to have Buddy Rich play on the album. But Buddy was under contract to Verve Records at the time.

Buddy Rich agreed to be "Buddy Poor" on Harry's new album. The name change fooled nobody once the first track started playing.

In my opinion, the drumming that Buddy Rich provided on the new James album, was the finest Big Band drumming Rich had ever recorded, outside of his own band.

On May 2-3, 1957, Harry James and his Orchestra recorded "Wild About Harry" for Capitol Records.

After sixty-plus years, "Wild About Harry" stands as the finest recording that Harry James ever recorded. His playing was beyond belief. The ensemble passages were as tight as any Big band.

There was a sense of renewal for Harry and everybody connected to his organization.

Buddy Rich left after the "Wild About Harry" recording session. But he returned for a stand at the Hollywood Palladium in preparation for the Harry James Orchestra's first European tour.

Harry James had received offers to perform in Europe before. However, with his new "Jazz" band, and Buddy Rich sharing top billing, the time was right to cross the Atlantic.

On October 8th, the James band left for Paris, France. For nearly a month, the band performed for sold-out audiences everywhere they went.

Audio from concerts in Hanover and Frankfort, Germany, shows the band was playing at a level few Big Band had ever reached.

Night after night, enthusiastic crowds encouraged the James boys and showed great respect for every member of Harry's entourage.

Buddy was happy. Harry was delighted and even opined that American audiences never reacted to or appreciated their music, the way that the European fans did.

On October 21st, the band played thousands of fans in Vienna, Austria. Cheers went up for each musician as they were announced on stage. That didn't happen in America.

From the first notes of "Ciribiribin," it was obvious that Harry James and his Orchestra were on fire!

The program featured a mixture of Jazz tunes from the late forties and fifties, pop tunes of the day featuring vocalist Jilla Webb, and showcases for the James band's soloists.

Herb Lorden had written an extended arrangement of "Sing, Sing, Sing," which featured Smith, Lorden, and Rich in over-the-top solos.

The band returned to Los Angeles in early November and made an appearance on "The Big Record Show with Patti Page" on November 13, 1957. Harry played "Ciribiribin," "You Made Me Love You," "Flash," and "Flight of the Bumblebee."

Corky Corcoran returned to Tacoma, and Buddy Rich left the band again to pursue his "singing" career.

Surprisingly little is known about lead trumpeter Don Paladino. In the liner notes to "Wild About Harry," Harry bragged on Paladino's playing. But he left the James band in early 1958.

Conflicting stories about Don Paladino have him dying at the age of thirty from a brain tumor. Another story had him being struck and killed by a taxicab.

Harry and the band took two months off before returning to the Hollywood Palladium in late January of 1958.

Las Vegas

Although the Hollywood Palladium continued to be the home base for the James band, Harry received offers from the rapidly growing Las Vegas hotels and casinos.

The band traveled up the California coast in early 1958, before returning to Hollywood to record another Capitol Record album.

Ollie Mitchell had joined the band as the new lead trumpet player. Jackie Mills once again filled the drum chair.

Corky Corcoran was replaced by Sam "Sonny" Firmature. Their playing styles on tenor sax were opposites. Corcoran being from the Hawkins-Webster school of tenor playing, and Firmature was from the Lester Young-Stan Getz school of jazz tenor playing.

Firmature was to be Harry's lead tenor sax for the next four years.

The relationship between Jackie Mills and his boss Harry James was always strained, to say the least.

Jackie Mills first joined the Harry James band in late 1949. Mills had a reputation as an excellent timekeeper and a very physical drummer. He had taken part in many of the Just Jazz All-star concerts and truly felt at home in any musical setting. He later became quite famous as a producer and recording studio entrepreneur.

Mills became the victim of Harry James' obsession with Buddy Rich. Every time Jackie Mills settled into the drum chores with the James band, Harry James would go off and chase Buddy Rich.

When the James band played opposite the Buddy Rich combo at the "Band Box" in 1953, Mills knew he was gone.

Yet every time Rich would leave Harry James, Mills got a call from James asking him to return to the band.

The Harry James Orchestra was a good paying gig for a drummer. And it enabled Jackie Mills to do other things while showing up at night for the James gig.

In interviews with Jackie Mills, it was apparent the Mills did not like Harry James.

In a 2009 interview, Mills said, "The band was wonderful...Harry James was not wonderful. He was a good bandleader, and he had a great bunch of guys. But Harry had an unfortunate ego."

I once asked who the best drummer that ever played with his band was. Harry replied without hesitation, "Jackie Mills."

The band entered the Capitol Records tower on April 1, 1958, for a three-day recording session for the album "The New James."

The band recorded an album of all originals again from Holman, Wilkins, and Hefti and Hill.

The session was also the first for new piano player Jack Perciful. Perciful had joined the band upon recommendation from Charlie Barnet.

Born in Moscow, Idaho, Jack Perciful joined Harry James in the Spring of 1958 and didn't look back until 1974. Over the sixteen years that Perciful has served as James's pianist, he had become close friends with Corky Corcoran and bassist Red Kelly. In 1974 Jack Perciful moved to Olympia, Washington, and, except for some tours with the Harry James ghost band, for the rest of his life stayed there.

Two of the tunes from "The New James" remained active in the Harry James book for the next twenty-five years. Those were "Just Lucky" and "One on the House."

In July of 1958, Harry James received an invitation for his band to appear in the Driftwood Lounge of the Flamingo Hotel in Las Vegas.

The Big Bands were beginning to appear in the front lounges of the Vegas hotel-casinos. These lounges served to keep serious gamblers closer to the gambling action than the big showrooms.

Harry James and his Orchestra were a natural fit from an entertainment viewpoint. And for the next decade, the names Harry James and The Flamingo were almost synonymous.

The Flamingo and the Hollywood Palladium combined to give Harry James a base of operations for his movie, tv, and radio appearances.

In June of 1958. Harry recorded another Capitol album called "Harry's Choice."

Aside from an updated version of "The Two O' Clock Jump" by Neal Hefti, and an exciting arrangement of "You're My Thrill" penned by J. Hill, the new Capitol album was all Ernie Wilkins.

Wilkins wrote a real flag-waver called "Blues for Sale," which Harry performed almost every night for the next twenty-five years.

Ernie Wilkins also wrote an arrangement of "Moten Swing" that was very close to the arrangement that Wilkins had written for Count Basie around the same time.

Harry James often fell victim to being "double-dipped" by arrangers. Most notable were Ernie Wilkins and Neal Hefti, who would write a chart for Basie, or Charlie Barnet, or some other band, then tweak a section here and there.

Then the arranger would sell it to Harry James.

Neal Hefti began the practice way back in 1948 when he wrote "Bluebeard's Blues" for Count Basie. Then he peddled it to Harry James.

The practice eventually caused an issue when the James band and Basie bands were to appear in the same venue.

Count Basie asked a couple of Harry's sidemen to "please let us play our tunes before you guys do!"

In fairness, Harry had arrangements of several Basie signature tunes written for his band. These included "Corner Pocket" and "Shiny Stockings."

Another interesting musical event occurred in December of 1958.

Crown Records, which was a relatively minor record label, started recording a series of "Tributes to the Big Bands."

For some of the albums, former members of the Dorsey, Miller, Goodman, etc., were added to studio musicians to recreate the original arrangements of the Big Bands.

Charlie Barnet's name was added to the title of the albums, although he denied even knowing about it.

Strangely, "Charlie Barnet presents a Tribute to Harry James," featured the then-current Harry James Orchestra, without Harry. The band laid down tracks for two such albums.

The first album, "Charlie Barnet presents a Tribute to Harry James," featured a young trumpet player named Rob Turk. Turk had played with Buddy Morrow, and Dick Jurgens' bands.

He was a great devotee of Harry James and understood Harry's style probably better than anyone.

The James band recorded several of Harry's hits and some of the more recent Jazz charts. Then Rob Turk came in and recorded his parts with the band tracks.

The second album produced by Crown with the James band was "Charlie Barnet presents a Salute to Harry James."

The trumpet solos on this album were played by Harry's old bandmate from the Ben Pollack band, Shorty Sherock.

Less than two years after the Crown albums, Ollie Mitchell left the lead trumpet position in Harry's band, and Harry offered the job to Rob Turk.

(Harry's first choice to replace Ollie Mitchell was Johnny Audino. Audino had played with Harry on some record sessions and a television appearance on the Jerry Lewis Show. However, Audino had been offered a steady gig in Las Vegas and turned Harry down.)

Rob Turk was a true workhorse. He was a student of Al Cass and used an Al Cass mouthpiece. But soon after taking the lead chair for Harry, he switched to a Parduba #1 model mouthpiece. (which is nearly impossible to play!) He felt he needed the smallest mouthpiece he could get to handle Harry's lead book.

Through the years, Rob Turk was a personal confidant of Harry, arranged a bunch of charts for the band, and even tried to tinker with Harry's mouthpieces to make them more satisfying to Harry.

Once asked about Harry James as a soloist, Rob Turk answered, "As a soloist, James was at his peak, and his former sidemen remember his musicianship with awe. "On a scale of one to ten," recalls Turk, "Harry was a fifty."

On October 5, 1958, Harry James and his Orchestra made the first of two appearances at the Monterey Jazz Festival.

The band performed "Ciribiribin," "Don't Be That Way," One on the House," "Moten Swing," "Just Lucky," "Blues for Ray (Sims)," and "Ultra."

The response of the crowd was tremendous and caused one to wonder why Harry wasn't more active in the Jazz festivals of the sixties and seventies.

The MGM years

In 1959, with the acquisition of Norman Granz's Verve Record label imminent, MGM began to sign Jazz artists to their MGM label.

Harry James agreed to a five-record deal with MGM in January 1959.

In January of 1959, the Harry James Orchestra recorded no less than fifteen tracks. Four of them were released as singles and never were issued on albums.

Two of the tracks, "Doodlin'" and "Proclamation," were never released.

The remaining eleven tracks were released on the album "Harry James and His New Swingin' Band." The lead trumpet chores were shared by Ollie Mitchell and Johnny Audino. Jackie Mills was on drums.

One of the tracks released as a single was "She's Got to Go." A Basie-Joe Williams blues "shouter," featuring Ernie Andrews. Andrews had joined the Harry James band in November 1958 while the band was performing at the Blue Note in Chicago.

There can be little doubt that Harry James viewed Ernie Andrews as his "Joe Williams." In reality, Andrews and Williams were quite different stylistically. However, it enabled Harry to play the type of tunes that Williams and Basie had been successful.

Ernie Andrews continued to tour occasionally with the James band for the next decade.

If possible, "Harry James and His New Swingin' Band" did more than "Wild About Harry" did to restore Harry James as a Jazz artist.

Nearly sixty years after it's release, Harry's solo on "Shiny Stockings" continues to baffle and amaze trumpet players all over the World.

Thousands of trumpet players have been called on to play the trumpet solo on Frank Foster's composition, written for the Count Basie Orchestra.

But Harry James didn't just play a solo. He seemed to be able to find every possible twist and turn imaginable from the familiar chord structure of "Shiny Stockings." Two-thirds of the solo is played above the staff. Yet Harry wasn't just screaming out high notes. Alternating between legato-tongued notes and firing off heavily accented staccato-tongued notes on his ascending runs up to high C. Playing passages in double-time, and all the while completely mindful of the chord structure.

This surely was an exhibition from a complete Jazz master of improvisation.

And just to prove that it was not edited, and re-edited recording studio trick, a radio broadcast from the Hollywood Palladium on November 20, 1959, shows Harry playing an even more incredible solo on "Shiny Stockings" than the studio version. He played, even more, double-time figures and threw in some "Bop" style licks.

For two decades after the release of "New Swingin' Band," Harry always enjoyed playing the lead trumpet part on the final chorus of "Shiny Stockings," usually lipping up to a full high F.

"Harry James and his Swingin' New Band" received a lot of radio airplay for several years after it's release. It represented such a departure from the Jazz public's image of who Harry James was.

Another track on the band's first album for MGM was "Deep Purple."

Neal Hefti the arrangement of "Deep Purple" in 1948, as a ballad feature for Harry, Corky, and Willie Smith. It was recorded two years later in June of 1950, for the Columbia album "Dance Date with Harry James."

Comparing the 1950 Columbia version, with the 1959 MGM version, demonstrates a stark difference in Harry James' approach to a ballad. For about five years, Harry often used a different style of vibrato, at least in recording sessions. Slower, and less intense, and very much in keeping with the "Modern" trumpet playing of the day.

Listening to Harry's solo on "Deep Purple" and his later recording of "Lover Man" on MGM showed an approach influenced by Harry's admiration for Clifford Brown.

Another example of Harry's gullibility in dealing with arrangers, the band recorded Ernie Wilkins' chart on "Cottontail" on the "New Swingin' Band" album.

A little digging into Big Band music turns up an arrangement Wilkins wrote for Count Basie called "Basie." It is pretty much the same arrangement, with tweaks to the melody line, and a sax soli passage. Only the lead playing of Harry James on "Cottontail" marks it as a Harry James arrangement.

"Cottontail" stayed in the book for the next two decades, often as a drum feature for Buddy Rich.

In January of 1960, Harry and the band went back to the studio to start work on the next MGM album.

The first track that was recorded was Ernie Wilkins' chart on Horace Silver's "Doodlin." Once again, Harry bought a chart that had already been used by someone else.

Wilkins wrote "Doodlin" for Dizzy Gillespie in 1957. There is no way of knowing whether Harry knew that or not. Harry and Dizzy were great friends, but that probably didn't matter.

It is also interesting that although there is very little difference between the Gillespie version of "Doodlin" and the James version, Harry didn't record the entire chart for MGM...this time.

The James band did record the entire Ernie Wilkins arrangement one year before, but for whatever reason, the take was rejected.

When Harry recorded "Doodlin" again for MGM in January of 1959, Harry cut out most of the entire mid-section of the chart. Thus, although James and Gillespie recorded versions are different, the actual arrangements were pretty close.

Another of the tracks recorded in January of 1959 featured trombonist Ray Sims as a vocalist.

Sims loved to sing, and he had a nice "regular guy" kind of voice. He did get to sing with the band on live dates and sang on a couple of albums with Corky Corcoran and brother Zoot Sims in the seventies.

By this time, drummer Jackie Mills had left the James band for the last time. He was replaced by Tony DeNicola.

Tony DeNicola was discovered after he left the Army band, by Merv Griffin. Griffin introduced DeNicola to his old boss, bandleader Freddy Martin. Martin hired Tony as his drummer and eventually was hired by Harry James.

Tony DeNicola was a much-beloved educator and had a long teaching and performing career until he died in 2006.

He added to the Harry James band a style of drumming very similar to Buddy Rich and was very much rooted in Big Band drumming.

Another major change came when Rob Turk joined the band as the new lead trumpet player. His style of playing the lead was very similar to Harry's playing. There are times when it was hard to tell the difference between Harry and Rob when the trumpets were playing a soli section.

Harry brought back his old buddy Jack Mathias to write a sentimental ballad version of "I'll Take Care of Your Cares for You." Frankie Laine recorded a version that hit the charts; however, the Jack Mathias version featured Harry at his most emotional, Sims crooning in his fashion, and a "glee club" patter featuring the entire James band.

Two weeks later, in February of 1960, the James band recorded a new album that featured a mixture of original charts and updated versions of Big Band classics.

The MGM album was called "Harry James Today," and although it did not have the impact of "New Swingin' Band" on the Jazz world, it presented a few "high points" in the recording career of Harry James.

Unlike many albums from which relatively few arrangements remain in the performing book, "Today" provided Harry James with no less than six tunes, which Harry continued to perform for many years.

Bob Florence only wrote three charts for the Harry James Orchestra. One was "Eyes," which was a swinging chart that featured Jack Perciful on piano, and Willie and Harry.

"Satin Doll," written for James by Florence, was a masterpiece. Harry always loved playing the music of Duke Ellington. "Satin Doll" starts with Perciful playing the familiar Ellington intro, followed by a rendition of the melody played by the entire band, with a response by Ernie Small on baritone sax.

Harry plays the bridge, and then after the band and Small finish the chorus, Harry plays a jazz solo.

Then the entire band, led by Rob Turk on lead trumpet, erupts, with DeNicola driving and filling with drum breaks.

The band reprises the melody, with Harry James taking over on muted trumpet and closing alone with the rhythm section.

"Satin Doll" became a staple in Harry's live appearances until the end. He also recorded it again in 1979.

The Ernie Wilkins arrangements of "Jersey Bounce," "King Porter Stomp," and "Rockin' in Rhythm" continued to be played by Harry and the band throughout the sixties and seventies.

Perhaps no arrangement from the 1960s made more of an impact on the Harry James Orchestra as did the Ernie Wilkins chart on "Take the A' Train."

The MGM recording of "Take the A' Train" showed the musicianship and power of the James band.

Starting with Jack Perciful's piano intro, which was then echoed by the muted brass section, the recording displays the precision and dynamic contrasts of the band's reading of Wilkins' chart.

After Harry's brief solo, Willie Smith delivers one of the recorded solos of his career.

Then the band begins to build throughout the rest of the performance. Harry then rides above the full band, until the tune comes to a quiet stop.

Soon after the MGM session, Wilkins added another section to the chart, which not only served to open up the chart for solos, but also for Harry to play an entire chorus. In live performance, Harry soon added his own lead trumpet part throughout the second half of the chart.

He would then usually play a solo showing off his technical skills as the band came to a stop.

In concerts for the next twenty-plus years, "Take the A' Train" never failed to elicit a rousing reaction from the audience. Harry and the band also recorded "A' Train" two more times. In 1967, and again in 1979.

Over the years, certain recordings by Harry James are held up as artistic triumphs for James.

The most cherished recordings from Harry's long career include "Trumpet Blues," "Ultra," "Brazilian Sleigh Bells," and "Tango Blues," all of which served to preserve Harry's skills and musical genius.

"Harry James Today" contained a recording that to many Harry James, provided the finest recorded Jazz solo that Harry ever recorded.

Ernie Wilkins' arrangement of "Lester Leaps In," is a tour de force for the entire James band.

After the exposition of the melody by a muted James and the band, there is a two-tenor recreation of Lester Young's original solo with the Count Basie Band. Then Sam Firmature and Jay Corre engage in a call and response exchange, which ends in their concluding together in two-part harmony.

After a roaring sixteen bar modulation by the Rob Turk led band, Harry begins to improvise over a driving rhythm section.

He embarks on a fourteen-chorus improvised solo, all on ONE chord, supported by a driving Tony DeNicola. Harry bobs and weaves, climbs and descends, through all the registers of his trumpet. Building and building to a thrilling climax when he hands the chart back to the band.

It is the longest Jazz solo that Harry James ever recorded.

Over the years, I have had people say that Harry somehow got lost in the "Rhythm-changes" of "Lester Leaps In."

Harry knew exactly what he was doing!

I have often imagined that if I were able to go back in time to witness any recording session in Harry's long career, I would want to be there to watch him lay down the solo on "Lester Leaps In."

Even the band had to watch in amazement!

September 1960 saw the Harry James Orchestra return to the studio.

They recorded what was to be the first of many arrangements by Rob Turk. The tune was "Theme from Orfeu Negro (Manha de Carnival)."

It was played as a somewhat dark ballad, with Harry rising above the band for the finale.

A brief guitar passage was played by Terry Rosen.

Terry Rosen was my friend and a wonderful guitar player. We worked together a couple of times in Columbia, South Carolina, back in the 1980s. I also to guest on his Jazz radio show, and of course, the topic was Harry James.

Terry related to me how he got hired to be the guitarist for the Harry James Orchestra.

In 1959, Terry Rosen and a couple of his buddies had a Rock band in Las Vegas. They were struggling to find work.

One night they had finished a gig and were driving down the Strip in Las Vegas at about three in the morning.

Standing in front of a Denny's Restaurant, leaning against a light pole, was a middle-aged man wearing a tuxedo.

Terry immediately thought that only a musician would be wearing a tuxedo at 3:00 AM in Las Vegas. He suggested that he and his friends should stop and ask him if he needed help.

The men pulled over to the curb and asked the man if he was ok.

The man told them that he was trying to catch a cab to the Flamingo Hotel.

As they were driving to the Flamingo, Terry asked the man what he was doing all dressed up and standing outside.

The man told them his name was Bob Poland, and he was playing saxophone with the Harry James Orchestra.

Terry told the man about their plight as young musicians. Poland said to Terry Rosen, "My Boss is looking for a guitar player."

Terry was somewhat skeptical.

Poland said, "No, really, we are rehearsing at the Flamingo this afternoon at three o'clock. Bring your guitar and come on down!"

Terry and his buddies dropped Poland off at the Flamingo.

Later that day, Terry thought about what is there to lose. So, he drove to the Flamingo that afternoon.

Bob Poland saw Terry walk through the door and went to meet him.

Poland led him to the bandstand and showed him where to set up.

Soon Harry James walked through the door. He made his way to the bandstand, without acknowledging Terry's presence. And called up a tune.

As Terry began reading the chart, there came a guitar solo. Terry played the solo and finished the rehearsal.

Harry started walking off the bandstand, looked at Terry Rosen, and said,

"Nice, Kid!"

Terry packed up his gear and started toward the door.

Bob Poland and Sal Monte came running after him, with Poland asking, "Where are you going?"

Terry replied that he was going back to his hotel room.

Bob Poland said, "Don't you know you just got hired?"

Terry replied that he didn't know that.

"What did the old man say to you?"

Terry said, "He said, 'Nice Kid."

Sal Monte said that meant that Harry liked him and handed him a contract.

Terry Rosen spent most of the next three years with Harry James and went on to become the guitarist for Sammy Davis Jr. and the Rat Pack.

Sadly, Terry Rosen died in December of 1999; his death ruled a suicide.

January 1961 brought a new recording session for MGM.

"The Spectacular Sound of Harry James" was an unusual mix of material. Side one was a "Suite" made up of compositions by Charles Albertine.

Charles Albertine was best known as an arranger for Les and Larry Elgart, Sammy Kaye, and The Three Suns, He was also the composer of Bandstand Boogie. He was a major composer/arranger for many television shows.

Albertine wrote five compositions for the "Spectacular Sound of Harry James." They were presented as a suite that tells the story, in musical form, of a love relationship.

In truth, although the James band played the material effectively, the content was not memorable enough to leave a lasting impression.

The "B" side was completely different, and memorable.

All of the charts were written by Ernie Wilkins. They are some of the best tracks ever recorded by Harry James and his Orchestra.

"Sweets Tooth," "Harry's Delight," and "Connectin' the Bones," were great Swing charts.

"The Jazz Connoisseur" showcased the power of the James band and Harry's technical skills. It remained in the book until the mid-1970s.

Ernie Wilkins' arrangement was another chart that Wilkins also recorded with his own Big Band, and featured Clark Terry.

Harry James showed the influence of Clifford Brown on his playing on "Lover Man." He used a slower and wider vibrato than he usually employed. He also played fewer notes than he perhaps would have on another ballad.

"Lover Man" is a testament to the versatility of Harry James as a musician.

Neal Hefti was one of the most talented musicians to come out of the Big Band Era. Hefti was a gifted trumpeter, composer, and arranger.

While still in high school, Neal Hefti began writing arrangements for various bands, including Earl Hines. In 1942, he wrote the famous chart for "Skyliner" for Charlie Barnet. After playing trumpet for the bands of Bobby Byrne, Horace Heidt, and Charlie Spivak, in 1944, Hefti joined Woody Herman's, First Herd.

With Herman's band heavily influenced by both Ellington and Bebop, Hefti quickly began writing arrangements for the Herd. Among his most famous arrangements were "Caldonia," "The Good Earth," and "Wild Root."

While playing the Harry James trumpet section briefly in 1949, Hefti started writing for the James band.

Harry was, in his way, beginning to embrace Bebop. Hefti was the perfect writer to meld Harry's brand of Swing with the complexities of Bebop.

As of this writing, several of Neal Hefti's arrangements for Harry James are now in print for today's college and professional musicians to play.

Harry wanted to produce an album of all Neal Hefti compositions.

"Harry James Plays Neal Hefti" is another high-water mark for Harry and the band. The compositions show all of the tools that were in Neal Hefti's writers' toolbox at the time.

"Chiarina" was written for the 1949 James band. The title was Hefti's wife Frances Wayne's real first name. (Her name was Chianina Francesca Bartocci)

James played "Chiarina" all through the sixties. Especially as a feature for the Buddy Rich driven rhythm section in the casinos.

"Sunday Morning" is a Gospel-tinged shouter, which is played to a twist beat. It features a muted James in a back and forth with the band. It soon was extended to include additional solos for Perciful on piano, James, and the alto sax of Joe Riggs.

"Tweet Tweet" became a favorite of Harry James. He played it until the end of his life. The same can be said for "Koo Koo." It features a section where Hefti's "Sixties twist" sensibilities are called out. (As a precursor for Batman!)

"Rainbow Kiss" became a closing theme for the band, enabling Harry to pronounce his gratitude to the audience, and to call out the soloists in the band, before going into "Ciribiribin."

"Harry James Plays Neal Hefti" garnered a large amount of radio airplay, as portrayed as perhaps Harry James's most Jazz-themed album.

It was during this time that Harry James and H=his Orchestra filmed their parts for a new Jerry Lewis movie, "The Ladies Man."

Jerry Lewis had a fascination with Harry James. Being a frustrated "Musician-wannabe," James and Lewis' paths crossed many times over the years.

In the "Ladies Man," the James band performs "Just Lucky" as background music for a scene in the movie.

Harry and the band also appeared in a bizarre sequence, where they appear out of thin air, dressed in all white, on a white set, and perform a shortened version of "Bangtail."

The following September of 1961, MGM tried to pull a fast one with Harry's next album.

Harry James and his Orchestra went into the studio to record an entire album of their hits.

With new drummer Jake Hanna aboard, Harry played "Ciribiribin," "You Made Me Love You," "Sleepy Lagoon, "Ultra," and eight other Harry James classics.

Then MGM combined an "action" photo taken at the Flamingo in Las Vegas, and an applause track added to the tracks to make it seem as though Harry had recorded a "live" album.

They called the album "Requests on the Road," to further give a false impression that this was a real "live" album.

The playing from Harry and the band was exemplary. However, the trickery by the MGM sound engineers detracts from the sound quality of the album.

In a 2006 interview, Jake Hanna spoke highly of his time playing drums for Harry James:

"Harry James was a great guy. He had a great band. It was like New Year's Eve every night. On the road, especially, Harry was a wild guy. He was the wildest guy in his own band.

He had Red Kelly there, that's total insanity. Ray Sims, Zoot's brother, he was there. Willie Smith, he was another New Year's Eve guy, that one was forever having a ball...we had a lot of funny guys, Nick Buono was there, from the original band. He was there forever. He was a real funny cat, a nice guy, beautiful!

Bud Rich came in after me. I went with Woody (Herman). Both bands turned out okay!"

Harry James had wanted to record an album of all Ralph Burns compositions for some time.

In July of 1961, the band recorded eight tracks for a proposed Burns album. But the tracks remained unissued until the 1990s.

One track from that album, "Moonchild," was lifted from Burns' three-part composition "Summer Sequence," which was so famously recorded by Woody Herman in 1948.

Jake Hanna was the drummer on the next Harry James MGM album.

The James band performed on the "All-Star Parade of Bands" live on New Year's Eve.

The radio broadcast emanated from the Flamingo with special guest Jimmy Rushing. The set included "Tweet Tweet" and "Sans Souci" from the Hefti album.

Harry played "Sleepy Lagoon," and Jimmy Rushing sang his signature song "Mister Five by Five." The set closed with the "Two O' Clock Twist," which was not a change of the arrangement, but a name change for radio.

Harry appeared on television and subsequent magazine ad campaign for Kleenex.

Harry appeared in a "live" sequence with a vocalist and a "stunt band," which included a young trumpet player named Herb Alpert.

In the ad, Harry played his trumpet with a wet Kleenex, purporting to show the strength of the Kleenex napkin.

"So strong that even the mighty Harry James can't blow through it!"

The ad was very successful for a couple of years, causing Harry to joke about it during an appearance on the "Hollywood Palace" in October 1964

.

The following week, Harry and the band returned to the studio to begin work on "The Solid Gold Trumpet of Harry James."

The album was another mix of retread James chestnuts, and new charts by Ernie Wilkins, Bob Florence, and Quincy Jones (probably ghostwritten by Wilkins).

The opening tune of the album was "The Opener" by Wilkins. It was designed as a follow up to "Get Off the Stand" from the "New Swingin' Band" album.

In the opener, Harry announced the soloists, including a brief drum solo from Jake Hanna.

"Autumn Leaves" was in the book from 1954 until 1983. Ray Conniff's beautiful arrangements of "Lush Life" and "Serenade in Blue" from the Columbia days are replayed.

Harry returns to his 1939 chart on "I'm In the Market for You," and, if possible, is even better performance than the original.

Harry and Willie readdress "I'm Confessin'," which is still a swing marvel.

The mutes came out for "The Mole." The arrangement of "Opus One" by Bob Florence stayed in the book until the end.

"Jones Beach," and "A Swinging Serenade," were only new to Harry, having been recorded by Wilkins and Quincy Jones.

Some pressings of the "Solid Gold" album featured the soundtrack to the Kleenex commercials.

This was to be the finale of Jake Hanna's career as the drummer for the Harry James Orchestra.

Bernard (Round Three)

Buddy Rich was convinced that his "heart trouble" was behind him. He called Harry James and said he wanted "his job" back.

Of course, Harry said yes. He called the band into his dressing room at the Flamingo Hotel's Driftwood Lounge and told them that Buddy was coming back with the band.

It is not known if Jake Hanna received any advanced notice, but the news from Harry signaled Jake's departure from the James band.

In truth, it couldn't have come at a more convenient time for Hanna. Nat Pierce had called him, offering him a job with Woody Herman's reorganized Big Band.

It is his tenure with the Woody Herman band that Jake Hanna is most remembered.

In February of 1962, Buddy Rich returned to the drum chair in Harry's band.

Almost from the beginning, this time, things would be different.

Buddy Rich would be treated as a headliner with the James band. The setting of tempos was no longer completely with Harry James.

Harry began to count off instrumentals MUCH faster than B.B (before Buddy).

Famed trumpet guru and former Harry James lead trumpet player once told me that he loved Buddy, but preferred playing with Sonny Payne on the band.

He said that when Buddy was on the band, it was all about Buddy!

Not long after Buddy returned to the band, so did Corky Corcoran.

This time Corky stayed for almost twelve years.

The next five years were the artistic zenith of the Harry James Orchestra. Harry was playing as well as ever, the rhythm section with new bass player Red Kelly, Jack Perciful, and Buddy Rich was without comparison. Harry was still carrying a guitar player, Dempsey Wright, at this point, but the guitar position would soon be removed.

Radio broadcasts from this period show the James band playing at an incredible level. The band personnel was to remain comparatively constant.

Buddy Rich still had health issues related to his heart but did not miss any playing time.

March of 1963 brought an opportunity for Harry James to do something that he had always wanted to do.

Record a Dixieland album!

The concept was the brainchild of former Bob Crosby clarinetist Matty Matlock.

Matlock had written a few Dixieland charts for the James band over the years. One of those charts was recorded by Harry on the "Juke Box Jamboree" album in 1954.

Matty Matlock and Harry discussed an album that would feature a "Dixieland Front-line," performing in front of the full James band. (It is not known if the concept was discussed with Mr. Rich, although he had plenty of experience in his days with Joe Marsala's band).

The "front line" consisted of Dick Cathcart on trumpet, Matty Matlock on clarinet, Matlock's former bandmate Eddie Miller on tenor sax, Ray Sims on trombone, and Harry James.

Dick Cathcart was a fine trumpet player in his own right. He had "ghosted" for Jack Webb in the movie "Pete Kelly's Blues." He had been a trumpeter for the U.S. Army Air Force Band and a member of big bands led by Bob Crosby, Ben Pollack, and Ray Noble. He also worked with Ray McKinley's band throughout the 1980s.

In 1962, Cathcart joined the "Lawrence Welk Family," appeared weekly on the Welk tv show, and eventually married Peggy Lennon of the Lennon Sisters.

New Orleans born tenor sax player Eddie Miller had been a member of the Ben Pollack band before Harry James was. He had a sound very similar to Bud Freeman, although he was noted for having a sweeter sound on ballads. He was a member of Bob Crosby's Bobcats, and also eventually worked with Pete Fountain, among many others.

The opening track for the "Double Dixie" album was "My Monday Date."

The first chorus featured Dick Cathcart playing the trumpet solo and lead. After Eddie Miller's tenor solo, there is a back and forth between the "Dixieland front line" and the full band.

As I sit here listening to "My Monday Date" on my stereo, there is a break, from which Harry James rises "ala-Satchmo" and plays majestically, both as a soloist and as lead trumpet.

Immediately upon listening to this album, it is obvious that Harry James is paying homage to his mentors Louis Armstrong and Muggsy Spanier.

There are two tracks in which Harry plays Louis Armstrong's solos, "Cornet Chop Suey," and "Weatherbird."

No other trumpet player after Louis could play these two tunes with the authenticity and power that Harry James plays with on this record.

"Squeeze Me" was a favorite of Harry's and was the only tune from "Double Dixie" that found its way into the James book.

In January of 1964, Harry James had to do something that he dreaded doing but had no choice.

Harry could tolerate drinking from his musicians, as long as it didn't affect the performance on the bandstand. To be sure, there were some World Class imbibers on the James band, of which Harry was the Chief!

The sad fact was that Willie Smith's drinking had become out of control. It affected his playing and his dependability.

Harry was forced to fire Willie Smith. That created a tremendous void in the James sax section.

Willie Smith's alto sax sound was almost as recognizable as the sound of James himself.

The band was in a rehearsal in the Driftwood Lounge at the Flamingo. There was silence.

Joe Riggs, who had played the second alto seated next to Willie for over two years, looked up at Harry and asked, "Who's going to play the lead?"

Harry replied, "You are!"

Riggs had been absorbing and learning from Willie Smith for two years. He proved to be the perfect replacement. When Joe Riggs finally left the band at the end of 1969, he was much harder to replace than Smith had been.

Joe Riggs was the new lead alto player for less than three months before he recorded his first album in that position.

The year 1964 was another year of triumphs and tremendous change in the Harry James Orchestra.

Thad Jones had been writing some arrangements for the James band.

Jones had been pivotal in the resurgence of the Basie band as a trumpet soloist. The fact is that when Thad Jones tried to write charts for the Count Basie band, Basie usually rejected them.

To Basie, they didn't fit the band's style. Thad Jones tended writing for a Big Band, with a small band mindset. At least that's what Count Basie thought.

So, in 1963 when Harry James let Thad Jones write some arrangements for his band, much the same thing happened.

Charts like" About Time," "Don't Min Us," and "Letter from Home," were tried in rehearsals at the Flamingo, and filed away.

Harry then asked Thad if he could write some charts for a few "Big Band Standards."

Thad came back with a few charts for the new band vocalist Ruth Price and some "old chestnuts" from the Swing Era...Thad Jones style.

Harry selected some of the charts, edited a couple, then added them to a couple of Ernie Wilkins charts that the band was already playing.

In March of 1964, the band recorded "New Versions of Downbeat Favorites" for MGM.

It was to be the final album with Rob Turk as the lead trumpet player.

As much as I love the performances from "New Versions," I believe that the album sounded rushed, and lacked the vitality that the earlier MGM albums had.

Highlights from "New Versions" were "If I Could Be with You One Hour Tonight," which featured Harry, and was one of the Thad Jones charts which Harry took a scalpel to.

"Sophisticated Lady" featured Harry and Corky. A raucous Jones arrangement of "Flying Home," from which Harry cut Thad's into completely off from the chart. And "Cherokee" which had so much promise as a chance to show off the sax section with the new "Joe Riggs" sound, and Buddy Rich.

An interesting fact about "Flying Home," is that there were two recorded endings for the Jones chart. The ending that Thad wrote featured a trombone section tag, that was somewhat difficult to execute.

The second ending was a brief Buddy Rich drum fill.

For some reason, MGM spliced the second Rich ending, on to the full recorded track.

So, some copies of the album had different endings for "Flying Home."

(In live performance, Harry turned Buddy Rich loose for a drum solo at the ending, before the band came in for the last note.)

During this period, Harry was struggling with adapting to his new dental implants. They would be a source of pain and annoyance for the rest of his life.

In April of 1964, the Harry James Orchestra, with vocalist Ruth Price embarked on a three-week tour of Japan.

The Japanese audiences adored Harry James and Buddy Rich.

While in Japan, the band recorded a television special. Set in a night-club setting, the band performed a mixture of James favorites and more recent Jazz tunes.

It was obvious that Harry was uncomfortable with his new teeth. Although he played well, as usual, he was holding back. I am sure that part of it was television production itself. Perhaps the Japanese television producers asked Harry and the band to tone it down.

I am sure that fatigue was part of it. The whole band had to be tired from the tour.

But watching Harry play, he seemed to be laying back. "September Song," for example, had Harry playing his solos with a cup mute. "Cherokee" was not the "barnburner" that it usually was.

Finally, Harry failed to play his high note passage on "Sleepy Lagoon."

Nonetheless, the tv program was well received and is well-worn viewing fifty-five years later.

One tune from the Japan tv show was "Cubano Chant."

Pianist Ray Bryant wrote "Cubano Chant," and it fast became a Jazz standard.

Arturo "Benito" Castro, of the famed Castro Brothers, brought Harry James an intricate arrangement of "Cubano Chant." Harry immediately recognized the potential in the arrangement, especially with Buddy Rich as the drummer.

On the Japanese television show, "Cubano Chant" was freshly added to the James book. Harry can be seen playing the melody in tandem with the trombone section. The trumpet section answers.

Harry's solo is good, but much more subdued than other recordings from the period.

The Japan tour was successful, by all accounts.

By August, Harry's chops were back to normal.

As the story goes, the James band had finished their last set at the Flamingo at about 2:00 AM.

Harry gathered a small contingent from his band and headed to the recording studio.

The group that recorded "In A Relaxed Mood" consisted of Harry, Ray Sims, and Corky Corcoran on horns. Jack Perciful, Red Kelly, Buddy Rich, and Guy Scalise on guitar were the rhythm section.

In one session, Harry and his small group recorded a set of standards.

The album served to display the sheer beauty of Harry James and his trumpet. Harry delivered his solos in a truly tasteful and soulful manner. It was probably the finest ballad playing ever recorded by Harry James.

"For All, We Know" is worth the price of the album.

Corky Corcoran plays "That's All" and played it virtually note for note, for the rest of his career.

Ray Sims on trombone, is just a joy to hear.

Jack Perciful remains, as this album illustrates, underrated as a Jazz pianist. Heavily influenced by Art Tatum, and Jimmy Rowles, Perciful should be known for much more than just being the piano player for the Harry James Orchestra.

For his part, Buddy Rich was equally tasteful and played session drums in a manner reminiscent of his playing with pianist Art Tatum twenty years before.

Harry's Chops (The Embouchure)

Of all the aspects of the trumpet playing of Harry James, few subjects have been discussed and analyzed as much as Harry's embouchure.

In case you are not a musician, the embouchure refers to the way you put your mouth on the instrument to make the proper sound.

As there are many trumpet players and styles, so are there many different embouchure setups. Although it is relatively easy to spot a "bad" or improper embouchure, there is no one single "right" way to blow a trumpet.

Any teacher, or musician who tells a student that there is only one "right" way to make a sound on a trumpet, is doing a considerable disservice to the student.

Lips are different. Dental structure varies from human to human. Some highly successful trumpet players have had to deal with big gaps between their front teeth. The great Jon Faddis is a good example of this.

Other trumpet players have had to deal with the loss of their teeth, and have had to learn to play with dentures, such as "Little Jazz" Roy Eldridge.

It has often been said that Harry James had the perfect embouchure. Close up photos of Harry's placement of his lips on his mouthpiece, have been used throughout the decades, to demonstrate the embouchure to young students.

In 1941, Robbins Music Corporation released a book called the "Harry James Trumpet Method." To be fair, Harry didn't have much to do with the book, as it was written by Everette James and Jay Arnold.

This is from the portion of the "Harry James Trumpet Method" directly dealing with the embouchure.

"It is rather difficult for a teacher to give a definite idea regarding the placing of the mouthpiece so much depends on the formation of the lips and teeth of each player.

Generally, the best results are obtained by placing the mouthpiece in the center of the lips using, if possible, two-thirds on the upper lip and one third on the lower lip. This can be reversed, however, with excellent results. The lips should, at all times, be in a smiling position. They must never be protruded; on the contrary, the corners of the mouth must be drawn down, enabling a freer, more open tone production".

That description well sums up the accepted embouchure training since the beginning.

However, that is not the embouchure training that I received from Harry James in 1970.

When I was sixteen years old, I didn't understand that I shouldn't ask technical questions of the World's Greatest Trumpet player!

To be honest, Harry didn't give a lot of thought about how he did what he did. He wasn't an "equipment" guy. It either worked for him, or it didn't.

When I first met Harry, I asked him how I could try and sound like him. He chose to demonstrate rather than tell me.

He reached into his trumpet case and pulled a mouthpiece from the small accessory compartment.

Harry handed me the mouthpiece and told me to place it on my lips, as though I were going to play the trumpet.

I put it to my lips, and he took his right index finger and pushed up on the center of my bottom lip.

Harry told me, "Put your mouthpiece two-thirds on your top lip, one-third on the bottom. This will help to keep your lips from rolling back. Your bottom lip is power—tongue through your teeth. Your tongue should act as an air valve.

"Most of all, breathe deep from your diaphragm. Breathing correctly is the most important part of a trumpet playing".

Harry took his deep, diaphragm breathing very seriously. Despite being a heavy smoker. Even into his sixties, he would "dare" people to punch him in the gut.

My wife, Cheryl, took that dare once. She's a strong girl. But when she punched Harry HARD in the gut, he didn't flinch.

Even late in his life, his breath control was astounding.

Harry James himself described his importance of proper breathing, as being the key to a successful trumpet sound. In the March 1953 edition of "Metronome "magazine, Harry told the following:

"I have found that breathing is the most important part of playing the trumpet. It appears that most trumpeters worry more about their lip, whereas they should concern themselves with breathing.

Naturally, the lip is very important, but in my opinion, the airstream passing through the lips into the trumpet is similar to the bow guided across the violin to produce the sound.

The sound, volume, and tone are the results of the pressure put forth from the diaphragm".

This is an appropriate place to discuss Harry's use and opinion on high notes.

Harry was one of the earliest trumpet players to play high note solos. For most of his career, Harry could play high F's and G's at will. Powerful high notes.

Even into the seventies, I witnessed Harry play double-high A flats and A's.

But Harry was not a fan of high notes just for high note's sake.

There was an example in the early seventies, when the lead trumpet player in Harry's band, put a couple of double-high C's, in a place where Harry thought it was inappropriate.

Harry turned to the player and said to him, "If you want to get into a screaming contest, get your ass down here right now!"

The lead player thought well not to take Harry up on his challenge!

Harry once told me that all trumpet players sound the same above a double-high G.

However, there was an exception.

The "Dot" Experiment

In 1964, Harry signed a record deal with Dot Records.

During the sixties, Dot Records made a specialty of hiring musical acts, who had been commercially successful earlier in their careers. Some of those names included Pat Boone, The Lennon Sisters, Louis Prima, Eddie Fisher, and the Mills Brothers.

Perhaps Dot was looking to find "lightning in a bottle" with many of those artists. Quite a few of the artists on Dot were Country and Western acts.

Armed with the knowledge that Harry James had been on the charts more than any other Big Band, they began to produce Harry's albums.

(Harry James and his Orchestra had 73 records in the charts between 1939-1955)

In 1964, Rob Turk left the James trumpet section. This allowed Harry to "upgrade" the trumpet section in his band to match the trumpet sections of Stan Kenton, Woody Herman, and Maynard Ferguson.

The James band was always looked upon as having "the best" trumpet sections for twenty years. However, with more modern bands and arrangers adopting a more brass oriented writing and performing style, Harry followed suit.

With his new Dot Records contract in hand, Harry decided to follow the same path.

Harry James admired and respected Stan Kenton greatly. He called Kenton and asked him for advice on forming a new trumpet section.

Stan Kenton recommended Tony Scodwell and Tom Porello. Tony Scodwell had been a member of the Kenton Mellophonium Band and was well known as a dependable lead trumpet player.

Tom Porrello had played lead trumpet for Kenton in 1963, and since the Kenton Band wasn't going to be touring as much in 1964, Tom joined Harry James.

This gave Harry James a trumpet section that had two lead trumpet players. Also, Tom Porrello's reputation as a premier "high-note" player, allowed the arrangers for Harry James to write more modern, and more technically challenging trumpet parts.

The first album that the "remodeled" James band recorded for Dot, was called "Harry James plays Green Onions and other Great Hits."

Tony Scodwell told me a funny story about the recording sessions for "Green Onions" ...

"The "Green Onions and Other Hits" was one that I got to do with Harry. We recorded it here in Las Vegas at a studio that backed up to the Union Pacific railroad tracks, and the union had an agreement to mandate a break whenever a train rolled by, which was quite often. Buddy walked in and threw a fit telling the engineer to remove ALL the drum mikes, and Harry agreed. He sounds pretty balanced on the final recording, though. Simpler times."

The album was a mixture of Jazz-oriented tunes that had been recorded by other groups, and pop-oriented ballads—all done with a rock-influenced beat, and plenty of screaming trumpet parts.

"Green Onions" was arranged by Rob Turk for the James band. However, to say that the chart borrowed heavily from the Henry Mancini arrangement would be an understatement.

Turk lifted the core of the Mancini arrangement, changed the instrumental voicings, and added a space for Harry James, clarinetist Bob Achilles, and Jack Perciful on Wurlitzer piano to solo.

The ending is virtually identical to the Mancini record, changed only by the addition of the James trumpet section led by Tom Porrello, with a quote from Gershwin's "It Ain't Necessarily So."

Attempts were made to have Harry James play in a style similar to the recordings by Bert Kaempfert. "Red Roses for a Blue Lady,"

"Three O' Clock in the Morning," and "Down by the Old Mill Stream," were blatant attempts at copying the Kaempfert style.

An extended version of Neal Hefti's "Sunday Morning," stressed the "twist" feel of the rhythm. Joe Riggs played an animated sax solo, then engaged in trading fours with the Maestro.

Rob Turk's arrangement of "Night Train" was almost "Sunday Morning Part two" in its attempt to entice dancers to Twist again.

Rob Turk figured prominently on another track on the album. He wrote the arrangement and played a trumpet duet with Harry on "The Lonely Bull" (Harry always announced the tune as "El Solo Toro.)

There are moments during "The Lonely Bull" where it is indeed difficult to tell which trumpet player is playing. Rob Turk sounded a great deal like Harry James.

In all, "Green Onions and other hits" failed to deliver its promise to make Harry James relevant to modern record buyers.

The next Dot album delivered more of the same.

"The Ballads and the Beat" featured modern, rock, and Latin style arrangements on one side, and "Harry James style" ballads on side B.

Recorded in September of 1965, the album had a couple of noteworthy tracks.

"Malaguena Salerosa" was a Mexican pop song, which has been covered by more than 200 artists since it was published in 1947.

Rob Turk wrote the arrangement for the James version of "Malaguena Salerosa," and it became a tune that Harry would perform for the next decade.

Soon after the Dot recording, "Malaguena Salerosa" became an extended chart during live performances. Harry would open the chart up for additional improvising for himself, and Joe Riggs on flute. Jack Perciful also often got to stretch out during concerts.

I saw Harry play "Malaguena Salerosa" twice in live concerts during the early seventies. He played longer solos, and allowed Dick Spencer to play solos, and engage in a back and forth with Harry.

"Going Out of My Head," also arranged by Rob Turk, remained a favorite of Harry's to play in live performances.

"I Never Knew" is a reprise of the 1953 recording on the Columbia album "Trumpet After Midnight."

Corky Corcoran and Ray Sims are the soloists.

Harry recorded "Willow Weep for Me" on the Capitol album "Harry's Choice" in 1958.

On the original recording of Ernie Wilkins' arrangement, Willie Smith was prominently featured on alto.

On the Dot version, Joe Riggs leads the sax section through the Willie Smith portion.

For me, the standout track from the "Ballad" side of the Dot album is "I Can Dream Can't I."

The Jack Pleis arrangement sounds like it could have been recorded in the 1940s. Harry's plaintive playing of the melody, with Corky Corcoran's lovely solo, offers one of the most emotional ballads of Harry's career.

The same month the band recorded "Ballads and the Beat," Harry accepted an invitation for the band to appear at the 1965 Monterey Jazz Festival.

Red Kelly was quoted as saying that the set by Harry James and his Orchestra at the 1965 Monterey Jazz Festival was "the best set I ever heard that band play!"

The premise of the performance was "A Tribute to the Trumpet." The trumpet players included Louis Armstrong, Dizzy Gillespie, and Miles Davis.

Famed recording engineer Wally Heider recorded the entire performance. It was always amazing to me that he never produced an album from those concert tapes.

James trumpeter Tony Scodwell wrote of the Monterey concert:

"The great remote engineer Wally Heider made tapes of the Harry James Band in 1965 at the Monterey Jazz Festival... I mean, no less than George Avakian called ME to offer his apologies for not being able to drum up any interest in these very rare recordings. [George produced Harry at Colombia along with some guy named Sinatra in their heydays].

We had obtained permission from Buddy Richs' wife Marie and daughter Cathy plus Ernie Andrews plus Jon Hendricks plus the James estate. That's how positive we all were that this recording should be released. Wally had given me 1/2 track dupes from the masters, and the missing segments were found in the Library of Congress [Wally didn't think I wanted the entire Buddy Rich solo on "Two O' Clock Jump]. The festival that year was billed as a "Tribute to The Trumpet," and we followed Satch, Clark Terry, Miles, and Dizzy. The band was amazing, and tempos were never faster. Harry, Ernie, and Jon Hendricks were all scat singing on "Flying Home." Amazing is an understatement for this recording. Do you see what I mean? It breaks my heart to have watched this all happen without a good result."

Parts of that recording found its way on to two "bootleg" albums on the Europa jazz label in the late 1970s.

It was not the entire set by the James band, but a significant enough portion to show that Red Kelly was right.

The set opened with the abridged version of "Shiny Stockings" that the band played from 1961 until 1983.

Then Harry and Corky shared the solo spotlight on "Sophisticated Lady."

Ernie Wilkins is featured on "Little Girl Blue," and "Ten Years of Tears," (recorded by Harry as "Trumpet Toast" for Dot.

The band plays "Caravan," "The Jazz Connoisseur," and "Green Onions," which featured Bob Achilles on clarinet.

Thad Jones's arrangement is given an eight-minute treatment. Jon Hendricks, Ernie Andrews, and Harry James take part in a scat fest, with Buddy Rich taking an extended solo.

The natural conclusion to that powerhouse set was a nine-minute version of the "Two O' Clock Jump" with a magnificent drum solo by Buddy Rich.

Many who attended that day at Monterey have said that the James band was the highlight of the Festival.

Also, during this period, Harry and the band performed on a television program called "The Great Bands" on WGN in Chicago.

Many of the most famous bands appeared in the one season program. The Harry James performance was divided between two episodes.

The WGN program was preserved on tape and has been distributed by Wally Heider on VHS during the 1980s, as "The Big Bands." Years later, a color version was discovered and continues to be sold by "Jazzlegends.com."

It is a marvelous example of the mid-60s Harry James Orchestra at its prime.

It also marked the final chapter of the Buddy Rich saga, at least as far as the Harry James Orchestra was concerned.

For his entire career, no matter how successful Buddy Rich had been, whether as a sideman or as a leader of a combo, it always came back to Rich's desire to lead his own Big Band.

At the end of April of 1966, Buddy Rich announced that he had had enough of being somebody else's drummer.

He was going to start his own Big Band.

This news did not take Harry James by surprise.

Harry asked famous session giant Alvin Stoller to fill a few dates with the James band.

Then once again, Louis Bellson returned to the James band. It was to be Bellson's fourth time with the Harry James band.

He told Harry up front that he would stay six months tops.

In all honesty, Louis Bellson was the best choice for the next two Dot Records projects.

The Riverboat

The Riverboat was a New York City nightclub that's name was an homage to Mark Twain. It was in the Empire State Building during the 1960s and 1970s.

It carried a description of "Home of the Big-Name Bands," which was the premise upon which the Riverboat operated through the end of the sixties.

The Harry James Orchestra held forth in at least two stands at the Riverboat in 1966. The Riverboat gave Harry and the band an anchor, from which they were able to make appearances on numerous radio broadcasts and television programs, including The Ed Sullivan Show and The Tonight Show.

Here is a good place to mention two appearances by the Harry James Orchestra on the Tonight Show starring Johnny Carson.

On October 1, 1964, Harry James and his Orchestra, with Buddy Rich, appeared on the Carson Show. They performed five tunes, which were "Shiny Stockings," "Cubano Chant," "Sunday Morning," "Caravan," and "The Jazz Connoisseur."

The James band made another appearance on the Tonight Show on May 17, 1966. This occurred during a two-week stand at the Riverboat.

This time, Louis Bellson was on drums.

The tunes performed were "Batman," "Michelle," "Afrika," "Two O' Clock Jump," and "Take the A' Train."

Unfortunately, when I contacted the Johnny Carson estate, who hold the Carson show broadcasts in an underground vault, they informed me that no film of those appearances had been preserved.

The third album that was recorded for Dot Records by the James band was "Live at the Riverboat."

The "Riverboat" album has been long cherished by Harry James fans for over fifty years. It offers a mixture of straight-ahead Jazz, ballads, and rock-tinged pop tunes.

When the James band was recording this album, many of the greatest trumpet players in New York City, came to witness the James juggernaut.

Doc Severinsen, Clark Terry, Marvin Stamm, and several others were online to witness Harry James and company.

The trumpet section for the "Riverboat" album was Tom Porrello, Carl Saunders, Al Yeager, and Nick Buono.

The entire album was recorded during sets at the Riverboat.

Lead trumpeter Tommy Porrello, who was ultra-present on the Dot album, described the recording to me this way:

"Chuck, "Riverboat" was recorded in 2 nights. All the nights, however, were 6 hours all week long. Quite a blow. Harry gave me the horn he was playing on this album, which I still have".

Tunes like "Batman" and "Do the Walk" featured much screaming by the James trumpet section.

Vocalist Ernie Andrews was featured on two cuts from the album.

"Gee, Baby Ain't I Good to You" not only showed Andrews' jazz singing skills but also featured Harry James on one of the greatest Jazz solos that he ever recorded.

Ernie Andrews also sang the Joe Turner blues classic "Roll 'Em Pete." Also featured on "Pete" was a rollicking tenor sax solo by Arno Marsh on tenor sax.

Longtime stalwart Corky Corcoran often expressed disappointment that he was not given solo space on the "Riverboat" album.

The album featured possibly the best-recorded version of Ray Conniff's arrangement of "Don't Be That Way," which also had Ray Sims solo on trombone and a drum break by Louis Bellson that showed that the band could survive and thrive without Buddy Rich!

The Rob Turk arrangement of the theme from "Batman," showed off all five trumpet players screaming with abandon in the last chorus.

However, for many James aficionados, the highlight of the "Riverboat" album, was the Rob Turk chart on "A Taste of Honey." Styled after the famous Herb Alpert record, the arrangement featured a fine Jazz solo by Harry and a spoof of the "Tijuana Brass" sound.

The beginning and the ending of "Honey" were what continues to be revered in awe by trumpet players and fans.

Harry James began "A Taste of Honey" with an improvised cadenza that is staggering in its execution.

He then played a cadenza over the shuffling rhythm section at the close of the chart. Harry then plays a double-high G that, to this day, remains legendary. Not that a double-high G was a rare occurrence, but the sheer volume, breadth, and scope of that powerful note played by Harry James, is staggering. As Harry released the note, on the recording, you can hear the echo in that night club!

Doc Severinsen described it to me in 1972, as one of the greatest trumpet performances he had ever witnessed.

During the May 1966 stand at the Riverboat, Harry James was featured on an Ed Sullivan Show broadcast. In one of those strange pairings that often came on the Sullivan show, Harry James sat on a stool, surrounded by the three McGuire Sisters.

The unusual combination performed a medley of Harry James, where once again, the many facets of the James sound were showcased.

Dots NOT connected

The next Dot album could not have been Harry's idea!

Dot Records had any number of "Country and Western" musical artists on the label.

Dot also managed to persuade several Non-Country artists to record "Country" albums, including Pat Boone, Lawrence Welk, and the Mills Brothers.

Someone convinced Harry James to record a "Country and Western" album.

(There were rumors that Buddy Rich caught wind of such an album, and it helped to hasten his exit from the James band!)

Harry took his versatile rhythm section, Jack Percival, Red Kelly, and Louis Bellson, into the studio on May 31st and June 1st, 1966.

Jimmy Haskell was a successful producer and arranger.

He was by no means strictly a "Country" arranger. His resume included many top artists from all genres.

He had arranged material for "Country" star Eddy Arnold.

He was called upon by Dot to create arrangements that would cover several types of "Country and Western" styles for the album with Harry James.

Haskell brought in a small string session, two guitarists, and a young session guitarist named Glen Campbell.

To be sure, Harry's playing was excellent throughout the entire album. The album was recorded live in the studio, without overdubbing.

It was indeed a kick to hear Harry James and Glen Campbell trading licks on "Mexicali Rose" and "San Antonio Rose."

Haskell wrote an arrangement of "Make the World Go Away" that was almost identical to the hit version recorded by Eddy Arnold. Harry liked it and played it for the rest of his life.

(He eventually recorded it again in 1976 for Sheffield Lab Records)

Harry also took a liking to "Blues Stay Away from Me." He had Rob Turk adapt the Haskell chart to fit his full Big Band.

The album featured an interesting album cover, featuring a painting of Harry in "cowboy" attire by Leo Jansen.

(Dutch artist Leo Jansen had also painted portraits of Raquel Welch, The Beatles, and The Rolling Stones.)

Though an interesting, if not failed experiment for Harry James, it did serve to show his versatility.

Louis Bellson's agreement with Harry had ended, and Bellson departed.

Harry struggled to find a suitable replacement for the drum chair.

(Rich and Bellson left immense shoes to fill!)

Former James drummer Tony DeNicola came in for a few dates, including an Ed Sullivan Show appearance.

Other drummers who auditioned were Charlie Persip, Sol Gubin, and eventual Lawrence Welk drummer Paul Humphrey.

The drummer that Harry James wanted was having problems of his own.

Percival "Sonny" Payne came by his drumming talent through his DNA. Payne's father was Chris Columbus, best known for his tenure with Louis Jordan.

Sonny Payne began playing drums with many of the "black" bands in New York when he was eighteen years old.

After spending three years working with the Erskine Hawkins band, Payne was offered a chance to fill in for Gus Johnson with

Count Basie's band. Johnson had undergone an emergency appendectomy.

Basie immediately saw that Sonny Payne brought a flashy, explosive style and energy to his recently reformed Big Band. Basie's popularity grew quickly during the mid-1950s, and Sonny Payne was a major part of it.

Throughout his adult life, Sonny Payne dealt with substance abuse issues. By 1965 his excesses had worn on his relationship with Count Basie. Payne began to become less dependable.

Basie and Payne departed in 1965, although he was in and out of the Basie band for about eighteen months. Frank Sinatra had insisted on Sonny Payne being "His" drummer, whenever he would work with Count Basie's band.

(There was a brief time in 1965-66 when Basie carried two drummers, Sonny Payne and Rufus "Speedy" Jones.)

Sonny Payne left his mark on the Basie band, and for the years after he left Basie for good, every successive drummer had to integrate a little bit of "Sonny Payne" into his drumming!

Payne had tried leading his combo in 1966, but he was too undisciplined to be a leader.

In December 1966, Harry James called Sonny Payne and offered him a job.

An "All-Star Parade of Bands" broadcast from the Flamingo on New Year's Eve 1966, showed completely different energy in the James band.

Sonny Payne was born to swing, and it was infectious!

The Harry James Orchestra showed a new spark and a new bounce.

Although some have criticized Sonny Payne as being too loud, and some have even questioned his timekeeping skills, there was no doubt that Sonny Payne was a perfect fit for Harry James.

James had to record one more album to fulfill his contract with Dot Records.

Harry James continued to want to record some Thad Jones charts. Dot Records was reluctant to have James record a "Jazz" album. They were still hoping to garner financial success for the remaining two albums of their contract with Harry James.

A compromise of sorts was found in May of 1967.

The Dot album "Our Leader" was a disappointment for several reasons.

Harry had included two Thad Jones charts in the album. "That's Thad" and "Don't Stop Now."

"That's Thad" offered a hard-swinging chart, with Thad's often strange voicings in some of the section writing. The tune bore some similarities to Ernie Wilkins' chart "Blues for Sale," with Harry opening the tune with a muted solo. Then Corky Corcoran plays a fine solo, followed by a sax section passage, with some unusual chord choices., led by the alto sax of Joe Riggs.

Then Harry comes back in, riding high above the band to the climax.

Perhaps it was the recording engineers' fault, but it just didn't sound right. It just seemed like it could have been better.

The only charts from "Our Leader" that stayed in the book were "On a Clear Day" with an arrangement by Rob Turk, and "Happy" written by Louis Bellson, and in performance usually featured Jack Perciful on piano.

All in all, the best that could be said of the Dot years was that they were good and bad.

The Dot recordings were not financially profitable, and except for "Live at the Riverboat," they never found their way into the canon of Harry James' best work.

However, Harry James was not finished.

The Golden Trumpet of Harry James

The 1960s found several "audiophile" record labels come and go.

These records were designed to enable audiophiles to show off their record players, especially those with new stereophonic systems, which was considered very cutting edge at the time.

Command Records offered great Jazz musicians like Urbie Green, Dick Hyman, Tony Mottola, and most noticeably Doc Severinsen, a recording outlet. The Command recordings were sometimes overproduced, and with too many recording gimmicks.

Enoch Light formed his record label after the sale of Command, "Project Three."

Decca Records followed suit with the introduction of their "audiophile" recording process "Phase 4 Stereo" and distributed it on Decca UK "London Records."

They recorded artists like Ted Heath, Ronnie Aldrich, Edmundo Ros or Stanley Black, and even Benny Goodman.

London Records offered Harry James an opportunity to record an album using the "Phase 4 Stereo" recording process in early 1968.

Though Harry was continuing to have issues with his dental implants, he agreed to schedule a recording session at Tutti Camarata's Sunset Sound in Hollywood, CA.

The London album consisted of several of Harry's hits and a couple of his sixties Jazz charts.

The album opened with the waltz version of "Ciribiribin," and closed with the new, upbeat version of Harry's theme.

Harry's playing was fantastic on the entire album. His solo on "Take the A' Train" was one of his better-recorded efforts.

I remember like it was yesterday, as a fifteen-year-old trumpet player taking my allowance to Musicland Records in Hialeah, Florida. The Golden Trumpet of Harry James" had just come out.

It cost me $4.98 plus tax.

I remember my Dad waited in the car to take me home. I ran to the record player and put the album on. My Dad explained to me who Corky Corcoran was, and recognized his solos on "I've Heard That Song Before," "Ultra," and "The Mole."

All through the album, I marveled at Harry James' hypnotic sound.

My friend Tony Scodwell told me a story about the recording session for "The Golden Trumpet" album.

"In 1968 I was playing with Harry James and we were scheduled to record the Phase 4 record called "The Golden Trumpet of Harry James," at the time state of the art was London Phase 4 and no less than Tutti Camarata was the producer.

Unbeknown to the band, Harry had full lower implants done four days before the recording. We sort of wondered why he was only doing one take on everything, but it was the road band re-recording his hits in a new sound, and we played everything all the time without thinking much about it.

The only thing Harry asked for another take on was "A-Train," which Harry soloed first and played some lead over the section on the out chorus. On the second take, Harry didn't play the lead part but got another good solo in, and we played through the entire chart minus Harry's lead.

Guess which take Tutti used?

Before the session started, Tutti asked Harry to "have the guys tune-up." Harry's response in a less than a kind way was, "this band just plays, they don't tune-up."

Maybe it was intentional, maybe not. One thing for certain, though, Harry played with those implants as nothing happened."

Dental problems or not, Harry James never sounded better!

Sometime in the early 1980s, the "Golden Trumpet" album was reissued on a label called Bainbridge Records. In addition to all the tunes from the London album, an unissued track, "Can't Take My Eyes Off of You," was included. The Rob Turk chart was an excellent example of the type of charts Harry was playing during the late sixties and early seventies.

Overall, "The Golden Trumpet of Harry James" was a testament to Harry's continued greatness as a bandleader and trumpet player.

The truth is that recording contracts for Big Bands, especially "Dance" bands were nearly impossible to get by the late 1960s.

Harry and his struggles with success

One of the great dilemmas that Harry struggled with during his entire career was that his Jazz playing skills could not propel him to stardom.

Harry James, at his core, was a Jazz musician. His early notoriety came from his amazing abilities as a Jazz soloist. He became quite famous as one of Benny Goodman's trumpet soloists. He only had to stand up in the trumpet section, and crowds would cheer uncontrollably.

So, Harry assumed, as did pretty much everybody else, that he need only start his own Big Band, and the strength of his blaring Jazz trumpet would be all he needed to become a star. From the beginning of his bandleading career, Harry James was pronounced as "The Nation's Number One Trumpet" and other sobriquets.

However, his Jazz trumpet was insufficient to reach the ultimate success as a bandleader.

Ah, but then he recorded "You Made Me Love You," and the die was cast.

The Harry James that I knew, and that many people knew, was a somewhat shy person. He had insecurities like all of us. He had a tough guy persona, that he created himself, to give him a feeling of belonging in the world of musicians. Most musicians, of which I am one, create a persona that is connected to our performing. It is the "person" that we allow others to see.

Musicians need the constant affirmation of applause of admiration because of our music.

That insecurity has ended, too soon, many a talented life.

But after recording "You Made Me Love You, "followed by a string of hits that dealt with sentimental themes, Harry became a celebrity.

Harry, the celebrity, was a quite different person, from Harry, the trumpet player. His celebrity status was only remotely connected to his trumpet playing. The higher his "Celebrity" star climbed, the farther it took him from his music, and musicians.

The young Harry James loved jam sessions and trading Jazz licks with his peers. By 1946, he was "Harry James-Hollywood Celebrity." He had pinups just like his wife, Betty Grable. He starred in movies and later television.

The celebrity status carried him through the 1940-50s. Then he began to cling to his Las Vegas life, which allowed him to engage in his self-destructive habits.

When the Vegas period ended, in 1972, Harry had to work. He had squandered his fortunes and truly needed to perform and tour.

The bobbysoxers were still around, but they were his age. He still played to sold-out audiences until the last. For them, it was nostalgia.

Harry James, like others, was musical "comfort food."

If there was ever a time that Harry James should have reached back to retrieve, "Harry James, the trumpet player." Famed jazz promoter Norman Granz tried to convince James to join in with his Jazz peers. Granz proposed a Jazz jam, and recording, which would have had Harry James to join with Harry "Sweets" Edison, and Roy Eldridge, Clark Terry, and Harry's old friend Dizzy Gillespie.

But Harry would have none of that.

The truth is, that although he was supremely confident in his trumpet playing skills, he was somewhat afraid to be compared to other trumpet players, even though they were his age.

Throughout his career, Harry refused to play tunes that had been connected to other trumpet players.

Harry never recorded "I Can' Get Started" (Bunny Berigan) or "Memories of You" (Sonny Dunham) or even "Stardust, (Billy Butterfield."

A perfect example of this occurred in May of 1968.

Harry and the band were on an East Coast tour. Ed Sullivan called Harry and asked if the band would like to participate in an "All-Star Salute to Irving Berlin."

There was absolutely no reason for any problem with that appearance.

However, there was a problem.

Former James lead trumpet player Tony Scodwell explained it this way:

"The 1968 Sullivan show we did was called a tribute to Irving Berlin. At the rehearsal, Harry called back to me, "catch my part

Babes," meaning Bunny's solo on the lead part. Harry put a fifth of Smirnoff away by 2 pm and another before the downbeat at 6 pm. Before the show, I asked Harry which part I should play, and once again, "catch my part Babes." Stupid and young that I was, I figured he was too juiced to play that famous solo. How wrong I was as you and I both know. He could've played it upside down and backward, but why they assigned him a piece made famous by Bunny was a bit of an insult, and Harry didn't do it. Certainly, he had recorded a Berlin tune in the past that could have been given him, and this was his way of reacting. Goulet being the "feature" might've added to it as well."

The truth is that Harry was no longer able to separate "Harry the Celebrity" from "Harry the Trumpet Player."

Harry had proven many times over the years that he was comfortable in a small group setting. He had recorded several sides with a combo and had even pared down to an octet for a couple of years.

But in the twilight of his career, he truly only felt comfortable with a fifteen-piece Big Band standing behind him.

He bragged that he often turned down offers to appear on television shows, but he said that they wanted him, not his band. He would say that he wouldn't go anywhere without "His Band."

With thirty-five years behind us, it is pointless to ponder his decisions. Surely, we would all love to have had recorded examples of Harry James trading fours with "The Trumpet Kings."

Human nature is what it is. Harry James was a simple, while also a complex man.

It just depended on which Harry James you were talking with!

Records and the Road

"The only commercial pressures I've ever had is when I have come up to do a recording date in the past few years, in which the companies have said to me: "Please redo some of the older things that you did in the early 'forties because now we can get it on the stereo and so forth, instead of it being only on 78s." And I wasn't happy to do it, but I thought: "Well, if there are people that liked this well enough to buy the records earlier, then they would like to hear them enhanced by modern recording methods." The same arrangements that are; I don't change the old ones. I have many, many new scores, but I figure that if someone wants to hear an old arrangement, they don't want it embellished or played in a different vein. They want to hear what they associated with it before. If I want to play something other than that, then I play new things. Because we have a lot of beautiful charts by Thad Jones, Neal Hefti and many other fine arrangers—you know, good jazz things. We have some good instrumentalists in the band, so we keep our spirits up by playing our new material.

I don't like to delve back to the more notable successes like "Trumpet Blues"? I used to enjoy things like "Back Beat Boogie."

They were such little things, you know, at the time. Playing that type of thing right now would not be satisfying to me. I would rather play Ernie Wilkins' "Blues for Sale," or something of the same type, that would have the same feel to it but that we would enjoy playing more, you see. Actually, "Back Beat Boogie" was just a head-arrangement. We just sketched out a couple of backgrounds, Dave Matthews and me.

The thing that we try to do now plays enough of the older things that people like so that they're not disappointed and, in the meantime, show the same people that we're capable of playing many of today's things. So, we hope they will leave saying: "Yes, I'm satisfied that they're still playing the music I'm familiar with, but also happy that they haven't been standing still."

Those comments were made by Harry James as he began to enter his fifth decade in which he led a Big Band. Things were changing in the entertainment industry, especially in the types of entertainment venues that presented Big Band programs.

November and December of 1968 brought Harry James and his former "boy singer "together again.

Frank Sinatra hired the Harry James Orchestra to appear with him for several weeks at Caesar's Palace in Las Vegas.

The billing would read "Bill Miller conducting The Harry James Orchestra."

Veteran Harry James and Las Vegas lead trumpet player Tommy Porrello, that the James band worked with Sinatra's rhythm section, with Irv Cottler on drums, Bill Miller on piano, and Al Viola on guitar. The complete James horn section performed intact.

Despite having left Harry's band in 1967, Harry would call Tommy Porrello whenever the band was going to backup Frank Sinatra.

Tommy Porrello is a legend in Las Vegas to this day.

In truth, there wasn't much for Harry to do.

One audio recording from the Sinatra show on December 5, 1968, has Harry James and His Orchestra playing "Two O' Clock Jump." Then Sinatra came out to do his show.

During the set, Frank Sinatra describes how he got the job singing with Harry James. Then the band begins the intro to the Nelson Riddle arrangement of "All or Nothing at All."

It does seem odd that Frank wouldn't have had Harry James play the original arrangement from 1939.

During the middle of the song, while the band plays Riddle's vamp section, Harry begins to wail in the high register. He continues to soar above the band until Sinatra closes out his vocal.

Frank Sinatra jokes to Harry by saying, "Too bad about your chops!" An obvious acknowledgment that, in Frank Sinatra's opinion, Harry James still had it!

Throughout the 1960s, Harry James had the comfort of knowing that he had steady work in the Nevada hotel-casinos. He had been able to call the "Flamingo" his base of operations. For twelve years, every tour, every television appearance would be coordinated with his shows in Las Vegas, Tahoe, and Reno.

By 1969, it became apparent that there were significant changes in the economy of Nevada on the horizon. New casinos were built off the Strip, Downtown, in addition to Tahoe and Reno. Las Vegas retained the largest portion of gaming revenue, but the clubs weren't as dominant as they had been in the late '60s.

The front lounges where entertainers like Harry James, Louis Prima, and many comedians, were being replaced by Keno and other games to increase gambling revenue.

It truly came as a shock to Harry James. It meant that he was going to have to change the way he booked his Big Band. It would mean more touring, often starting in Texas, and ending up in New York, or Florida.

It meant that Harry James would have to replace Las Vegas shows, with high school and college concerts.

Some of the musicians who had been with Harry for years did not want to spend months every year on the road and riding on buses.

Ray Sims had been the trombone voice in Harry's band since 1957. He was the first musician to hand Harry his notice of resignation in 1969. Sims had had enough of the road and preferred to settle down and play when he felt like it.

Joe Riggs decided to leave the band to tour less and work in the house bands in Las Vegas. His departure hit Harry the hardest. After losing Willie Smith in 1963, Joe Riggs stepped in and lifted the James sax section on his shoulders. His sound had become synonymous with Harry James.

Pianist Jack Perciful remained, so did Corky Corcoran. However, Harry was forced to replace seasoned veteran players, with younger musicians. Some fresh out of college.

The last recording sessions for the great 1960s Harry James Orchestra were for an unlikely record company.

Readers Digest had decided to follow the "designer" labels, which predominantly were sold through the mail. You couldn't walk into a record store and buy a "K-Tel" album, or a "Readers Digest" recording. You saw an ad in a magazine, or on television, you filled out an order form, attached a check or money order, and mailed it in.

In 1959, Readers Digest started into the record business by putting together compilation sets of materials that had been recorded in the decades before. Some of the titles were "Popular Music Hit Parade," and "Mood Music for Listening and Relaxation," and "   The Great Band Era (1936-1945)," (my Dad and I wore that one out!)

In 1969, Readers Digest asked several of the best-known Big Band leaders from the forties, to record "Swing" versions of modern pop songs, and to reprise some of the old hits. Some of the leaders didn't even have a band anymore, such as Charlie Barnet and Bob Crosby. Others like Duke Ellington, Les Brown, and Benny Goodman, were asked to record songs that were far beneath their usual music.

Harry James was asked to take part in the "Readers Digest Sessions," and fared better than his fellow bandleaders in choice of material.

Largely due to the wonderful writing of Rob Turk, songs like "Traces," and By the Time I Get to Phoenix," and "Gigi," were excellent choices for Harry James to play.

There are some inconsistencies with the recording details of the "Readers Digest" recordings. Some of the tracks were recorded by Harry's band, although some of the personnel is questionable.

A significant number of the recordings were recorded using musicians from England. It is undetermined as to whether Harry recorded these tunes with the musicians, or whether he overdubbed band tracks back in Hollywood.

Former James vocalist Helen Forrest came back to record several songs, both with Harry James and with Alan Copeland and a studio orchestra.

The relationship between Harry James and Helen Forrest was strained. There were deep feelings on Helen's part, and they included resentment, anger, and pain, due to the way that there love relationship had ended in 1943.

As a result, Harry and Helen had not appeared together in performance since 1944.

In 1958 when Harry James and his Orchestra and Helen Forrest were guest stars on the television show "The Big Record with Patti Page," Harry walked away from the set when Helen came out to sing "I Don't Want to Walk Without You." When she gracefully left the camera, Harry returned to play "Brazilian Sleigh Bells."

In May of 1969, Helen and Harry recorded four of their big hits. Also, there were four more recordings with the two of them, and the Harry James Orchestra plus strings. These recordings were made in RCA Studios in Hollywood.

(The recording dates vary depending on the source. Charles Garrod listed three different sessions over two years in his "Harry James Discography," including some in late 1971. However, the Helen and Harry pairings seem to me to have been in 1969, because I still hear Joe Riggs in some of the tracks.)

Helen Forrest never sounded better than she did on these tracks.

Despite dental problems, decades of smoking and drinking, and, being a road warrior, Harry James' tone was huge on these recordings.

"I've Heard That Song Before" was a shortened arrangement, with Harry playing half of the original solo. Corky Corcoran reprised his memorable solo from the 1942 recording.

Of course, Helen Forrest was not the vocalist on the original 1944 record of "I'm Beginning to See the Light," that was Kitty Kallen. But Helen did sing the Capitol version in 1955.

The version of "I Had the Craziest Dream" that they recorded not only shows Harry and Helen still vibrant artists, but the instrumental section leading to Helen's closing vocal shows the beauty and power of Harry's lead trumpet.

"I Don't Want to Walk Without" is even more poignant than the original, with Harry's emotional trumpet playing in a pleading style.

Harry and Helen appeared on an ABC television series in June of 1970, called "Happy Days." The show, not to be confused with the later television series starring "The Fonz," was an attempt to recreate 1930s radio broadcasts, with comedy skits emulating stars of the thirties, such as Laurel and Hardy, etc.

Each week a different Big Band leader appeared, fronting a studio band.

Harry appeared on two of the shows, with Jack Perciful, Corky Corcoran, and Sonny Payne performing with a studio band.

Once again, Helen Forrest sang her hits from the James days, but without Harry appearing with her.

There are some moments from the Readers Digest sessions that are quite memorable. Others are slightly off the mark. Harry's trumpet sounded great on all of the tracks. He played with tremendous vigor and strength.

There was a period in 1969 when Harry was struggling with his trumpet section. Garrod listed what he thought the personnel to be during this time. However, I have heard several different versions of exactly who the trumpet players were on these recordings.

The recordings that were made with Harry's band showed an uneven sound in the trumpet section. Some of the spots almost sound like whoever the lead trumpet was, played into a separate microphone, and was out of tune.

The trombone section with Ray Sims leading, the saxophone section led by Joe Riggs and Corky Corcoran, sounded great as always, and the rhythm section with Jack Perciful on piano, possibly Chuck Lawson on bass, and Sonny Payne on drums is outstanding.

The Ernie Wilkins arrangement of "King Porter Stomp" omits Harry's opening solo and replaces it with a four-bar break from Sonny Payne. Corky Corcoran and Ray Sims both solo, but it is Harry's solo that stands out.

Harry enters with a lip glissando up to a double-high G. Then, he plays an "all-out" Jazz solo ending on another glissando up to a high E flat. Then in the final chorus, Harry takes the lead in the trumpet section with power.

Harry also plays the lead in the trumpet section passage in "Music Makers." Again, the trumpet section without Harry sounds uneven.

Bob Florence's arrangement of "Opus One" had changed a little since the 1961 MGM recording. Harry kicked it off at a much brisker tempo. Corky solos and Harry plays a great solo.

It is interesting to hear the 1969 version of Harry James and his Orchestra play the old warhorse "Back Beat Boogie." Whereas the

1939 version featured a biting, muted James solo, this version has Harry playing very aggressively. He bounces around in the high register, showing that his chops were still solid.

"A Taste of Honey" has a much different feel than the "Live at the Riverboat" version. "Honey" is what you would have heard when Harry would play it in a dance set throughout the 1970s. No opening cadenza, and ending on a high D instead of a double-high G.

Rob Turk wrote the charts for "By the Time I Get to Phoenix" and "Traces." Harry played "Phoenix" often during the early seventies.

"Traces" had been a recent hit, at that time, by Dennis Yost and the Classics IV. Somehow, the song touched a nerve in Harry James.

Harry once told me that when he played a ballad, he would be thinking of the lyrics as he played. The lyrics for "Traces" brought memories of his love and marriage to Betty Grable. Though their marriage had ended in 1965, there could be no doubt that they still loved each other.

The first time I saw Harry perform in January 1970, Harry played "Traces" twice during the four-hour dance date in Miami, Florida.

Harry played "Traces" regularly up to his death. He recorded it again for Sheffield Lab in 1976.

Harry James recorded in total forty-six tracks for Readers Digest. I have tried, in vain, for decades to obtain the session records for the recordings.

Many of the tracks were not record with Harry's band. Because it is known that Harry made three trips to England from 1970-1972, perhaps these tracks were recorded then.

There are saxophone solos on some of the tunes that sound like tenor sax player Bob Efford. For sure, they are not made by Corky Corcoran.

I have been told that Harry may have recorded his portions of these tracks in Hollywood, overdubbing the orchestra tracks from England.

Regardless, these recordings show that Harry James was still an amazing player.

There are a couple of standout tracks on the Readers Digest Sessions.

Harry loved to play ballads in the key of D concert, (his key of E, not a trumpet player's favorite Jazz key!).

Rob Turk's gorgeous arrangement of "I'll Be Seeing You, "played in the key of D concert, starts with Harry playing in a very rubato fashion. He renders the melody in a very emotional style.

He shows off his full lower register throughout most of the performance, until after the tenor sax solo. Then Harry works his way up to the high register, finishing with a high F sharp, hanging out there, all by himself. Then the orchestra finishes with a James trumpet flourish.

The recording of "I'll Be Seeing You" was transcribed over forty years later, and the arrangement is still available to purchase on the Internet.

"Fly Me to the Moon" and "Around the World" show Harry showing off his upper range.

The Rob Turk arrangement of "Gigi," is one of the most striking recordings of James' career.

It offers a final recorded example of the musical relationship between Harry James and tenor saxophonist Corky Corcoran.

Corky starts the tune with a solo passage, leading to the entrance of the band, and Harry. Harry engages in a back and forth rendering of the melody until the end, which has Harry playing a passage showing his breath control to full advantage.

"Gigi" got played quite often until Corky Corcoran left the band. There is no record of Harry ever calling up the tune again.

All in all, the Readers Digest sessions are truly some of Harry James' best work. Though not commercially successful.

Female vocalists tended to come and go with the James band. A handful stood out, including Helen Forrest, Kitty Kallen, and Ruth Price.

From 1969-1971, the Harry James Orchestra featured a vocalist named Cathy Chemi. Chemi sang with a very strong feel. Yet at times delivered ballads with a powerful voice reminiscent of Eydie Gorme and Vicki Carr.

A New Year's Eve "All-Star Parade of Bands" remote from December 31, 1970, features Cathy Chemi singing "Didn't We." Anyone who heard that broadcast had to ask themselves why Cathy Chemi didn't go on too much bigger and better things.

She eventually married one of Harry's trumpet players, Skip Stine, and settled in to be a performer and educator in Eastern Pennsylvania.

Harry and the band played a couple of cruise ships for the Sitmar Cruise Line

Cathy Chemi and Skip Stine, along with vocalist Glen Ray were part of the band that toured Europe in the Fall of 1970.

Harry James had not been to Europe since 1957. Although there were many offers over the years.

The band performed in England, Denmark, Scotland, Italy, and Germany, to packed houses.

A video of a concert from the Tivoli Gardens in Denmark shows Harry James and His Orchestra at the top of their game.

The James rhythm section, consisting of Jack Perciful on piano, Sonny Payne on drums, and John Smith on bass, managed to stay intact for almost three years.

The saxophone section was less by Bill Byrne on alto. Byrne is well known in the West Coast Jazz community as having played baritone sax for several Big Bands. Byrne replaced veteran clarinetist Gus Bivona, who filled in for a short time after Joe Riggs left.

Veteran James sideman Don Mohr played second alto sax.

Corky Corcoran and Gary Herbig were the tenor sax players. Herbig later recorded extensively with many artists across the spectrum of Jazz and Pop. Jack Watson played baritone sax.

The trombone section was led by Harry's old pal Dave Robbins. Robbins was a brilliant trombonist/writer/arranger, who served multiple tours with Harry James, starting in 1949.

Dave Robbins was a beloved educator in Vancouver, British Columbia. He was a soloist of great style and humor, and he loved throwing musical curveballs at Harry James.

The other trombonists were Bill Payntor and Gail Martin on bass trombone.

The trumpet section included Thomas Holden, Jack Poster, Clarence "Skip" Stine, and Skip Pfyle.

It was obvious from the opening bars of "Don't Be That Way," that the Danish audience held Harry James, and the American musicians, in a place of awe and high respect.

Harry was in rare form throughout the entire concert. Several of the tunes performed, including "Take the A-Train," "Corner Pocket, "and Sly and the Family Stone's "Dance to the Music" showed off Harry's upper register chops.

Glen Ray sang a couple of "Vegas-style" vocals.

Cathy Chemi brought the house down with her vocals on "Didn't We," and "Summertime."

Harry played his always beautiful solos on "Sleepy Lagoon." When Dave Robbins played the trombone solo on "Sleepy," he ended the tender solo with a decidedly "roadhouse" blues lick, which amused Harry so much that he struggled to regain his composure in time to finish his solo.

During the afternoon of the concert, Harry and Corky spent several hours with tenor sax great Ben Webster...drinking.

(Corky Corcoran idolized and emulated Ben Webster.)

Throughout the concert, it was apparent that Corky had perhaps had too much to drink.

After Harry and the band had finished playing Duke Ellington's "Rockin' in Rhythm," Harry invited Ben Webster on stage to say a few words. Webster was intoxicated, and his speech was rambling. Several people in the audience began booing and taunting Webster.

Harry chided the audience, telling them, "I think the great thing about music in the whole world, is that we never lose our love for the people that we've known for so many years. And we admire and love their talents, believe me!"

The James band closed the performance with the obligatory "Two O' Clock Jump, "and the closing" Ciribiribin."

After Harry walked off the stage, the standing ovation, and the accompanying cheers, applause, and foot-stomping, he returned to play two more encores.

The band plays Ernie Wilkins's arrangement of "Cottontail" with section passages playing homage to Ben Webster's solo on the 1940 Ellington recording.

Then Harry returns to the stage and kicks off "Blues for Sale," showing off Corky, Dave Robbins in a plunger solo, and Harry soaring to the end.

It is truly a treasure to have the video record of this amazing concert.

The band returned to the United States and finished 1970 with a stand at the Desert Inn in Las Vegas. Singer Billy Daniels was also on the bill with Harry.

In January of 1971, the Harry James Orchestra played a Southern tour, starting in Florida.

I was able to spend some time with Harry during that tour, as I have detailed in the "Harry and Me" portion of this book.

At the end of the Southern tour, Cathy Chemi and Skip Stine left the band. Vocalists Cathy Carter and Sandy Moffat filled in for the next tour in May of 1971.

Upon returning to Las Vegas in the Summer of 1971, vocalist Rita Graham joined the band. She had been singing with Ray Charles, and Charles produced an album for her.

She joined the band at the Desert Inn in Las Vegas and was with the band until the beginning of 1973.

Rita Graham was the vocalist with the James band when it embarked on another European tour.

In September and October of 1972, James toured Europe, including a landmark concert at Royal Festival Hall, and television broadcast on the BBC called "Sounds for Saturday."

A video record of that concert is one of the best concerts that the Harry James Orchestra ever gave.

The entire concert can be viewed on YouTube and is a great way to spend an hour.

The performance of "Trumpet Blues" is an amazing example of Harry's trumpet skills as he was in his mid-fifties.

The Thad Jones composition "More Splutie, please" had been in the James book since 1963. Harry played it as an upbeat tune through the late sixties. However, by 1970, it had settled into a medium tempo blues, featuring Jack Perciful on piano, Harry, and Dave Robbins on trombone.

Harry's playing on the 1970 and 1971 videos from Europe, show him to be a master of the blues still.

While in England, Harry James recorded an album for the Longines Symphonette label. Longines Symphonette was a Classical Music label, who followed the Readers Digest record label in introducing Jazz and Pop into their catalog.

The premise of Harry James' involvement with Longines Symphonette, was that they were going to release "Remastered" versions of Harry's Capitol Records output. The James tracks were released in a five-record set called "Dance Band Spectacular." The problem with the records was that the "Remastering" process resulted in the tracks being one half step sharp in pitch.

The entire collection resulted in selling Harry's Capitol recordings in the wrong key. This was probably not a problem for most of the people who bought the record set, but for me, as a musician, they were unplayable.

When the mail-order Longines Symphonette label ran their advertising in magazines, they offered a "bonus" LP.

The "bonus LP" was called "Mr. Trumpet- Harry James Salutes the Great Trumpet Men of Our Times." Although Harry had usually refused to cover tunes that had been identified with other trumpet players, he did perform several songs that had been in the repertoire of Louis Armstrong, Ziggy Elman, Sweets Edison, and Henry Busse.

Harry made no attempt to recreate the original versions but asked Rob Turk to write some charts of tunes those trumpet greats were identified with.

The "Mr. Trumpet album was recorded while Harry James and his Orchestra were performing their European tour. Rather than a record with the James band, Harry recorded with a Big Band made up of some of England's best studio musicians.

There are some problems with the accuracy of the recording dates and band personnel.

I have heard from several musicians who were in the historical sessions, all of whom were in awe of being in Harry's presence, and for the opportunity to record with him.

Based upon what little research that I have been able to do, the band included Tony Fisher and Greg Bowen were among the trumpet players. Legendary trombonist Don Lusher was joined by trombonist Ray Premru.

Bob Efford was the tenor sax soloist, in addition to Ray Swinfield, Keith Bird was among the sax players.

Ronnie Price was the pianist, and Kenny Clare was the drummer.

Studio notes credit Geoff Love as being in charge of the sessions.

Two of the charts on the album had been in the James book for twenty years. "Don't Be That Way" was the opening tune to most Harry James performances since 1952. Matty Matlock wrote the arrangement for "Jazz Me Blues" in 1952. It was played quite often in Harry James's performances during the early fifties, and Harry played it in the Universal Music short "Leave it To Harry" in 1953.

The highlight of the "Mr. Trumpet" album was Rob Turk's arrangement of "The Sheik of Araby."

On the studio recording, Harry starts with a four-bar "stop-time" break, from which he takes the lead with the Dixieland instrumentation.

After the first chorus, veteran tenor sax player Bob Efford takes a full chorus.

Harry takes a chorus in true Dixieland style, then the full band comes in, with Harry supplying four-bar breaks. Then tune ends with Harry riding over the whole band.

"More Than You Know," "Indiana," and "When It's Sleepy Time Down South," were handled in a rather "James-like" ballad approach.

Several reviewers of the "Mr. Trumpet" album, have expressed disappointment at the brevity of the album. It does clock under thirty minutes. Also, the album was not as widely circulated as traditionally released Jazz albums. It became more well known when Hindsight Records reissued it in 1994.

Nonetheless, it is a great record of how well Harry was still playing in the early 1970s.

Going through the Motions

Although Betty Grable had divorced Harry James in 1965, they still carried a torch for each other. Perhaps in dreams of what might have been.

Betty Grable died on July 2, 1973.

From that day forward, Harry James was never the same.

The band was still playing to sold-out audiences on nationwide tours. Although Harry was still playing very well on many nights, there were nights when Harry's heart wasn't in his playing.

Each time that I saw Harry and the band, I was never disappointed. Yet I knew when he was just going through the motions. The audiences didn't know the difference and were always appreciative of how his music could still evoke wonderful memories.

One of those nights was in Miami in 1974. I got to spend a few moments with Harry. However, after each set at the dance date, he went to his dressing room, instead of talking to people or even going to the bar.

He played beautifully. Yet I knew that he was just going through the motions. He obviously couldn't wait for the gig to end.

During this time, Harry often appeared with his friend Phil Harris in Nevada casinos. Some of these shows added Frank Sinatra Jr.

James and Harris also appeared on the 1975 Jerry Lewis Muscular Dystrophy Telethon.

Jerry Lewis seemed to think that engaging in a "trumpet duel" with Harry James was uproariously funny. He did it several times over the years.

In July of 1974, famed promoter George Wein moved his "Newport Jazz Festival" to New York City. Rather than being staged at one venue, as in the past, the Newport Jazz Festival was presented at several venues.

Wein had asked Harry James time and again to appear at Newport. Yet money and touring conflicts never allowed the opportunity.

On July 2, 1974, Harry James and his Orchestra took the stage at Carnegie Hall for a concert. Harry shared the stage with Lionel Hampton and his Orchestra, and Buddy Rich and his band.

An audio recording of the concert showed that Harry and his band were feeling the emotions of Harry returning to the stage where he became famous with Benny Goodman in 1938.

George Wein introduced Harry by saying, "In the twenty-one years that we've had the Newport Jazz Festival, we've never had the opportunity to present Harry James. But we did last night at the Roseland Ballroom, and he was wonderful.

"Tonight is an even more historic occasion. Let's welcome him out here. Harry James and the Orchestra!"

Harry was at his best that night. In the program, Harry and the band played "Ultra" as the third number, in place of "Shiny Stockings" as he usually did.

Corky Corcoran had left the band in 1973. However, Harry knew of the importance of the concert and invited Corky to return as a "special guest" soloist. Corky was featured on "Alone Together," and then on an extended, seven-and-a-half-minute version of "Caravan."

Les DeMerle was the band drummer at that time. DeMerle had been on and off the band since 1970, and into the 1980s.

He wrote these remarks while remembering that night.

"We changed the arrangement on that number and played another tune in the middle of my solo on "Apples" titled "Louie Rides Again." Louie Bellson gave me this chart as a gift, and I brought it to Harry as we rehearsed on a Big Band Cruise a few weeks before our east coast tour was to start. I asked Harry if we could insert this tune in the middle of my solo on "Apples" at Carnegie Hall, and Harry agreed. The fiery tenor sax solo on the rock section of this piece is by Eddie Easton, who could play up a storm.

Another very special surprise that night in 1974 at Carnegie Hall happened just as the curtain went up after George Wein's introduction when I saw my parents in the box seats closest to stage right. My Mom and Dad had taken a Greyhound Bus from LA to NY just to see and hear me with Harry James at Carnegie Hall. This night playing with my main man and mentor, Harry James, and opening for my hero, Buddy Rich, with my parents in the audience, was one of the highlights of my life!"

The audience was especially appreciative of the James band's program.

In his closing remarks, George Wein said, "It took us 21 years to get Harry James here, but I already talked to his manager, and he'll be back next year for the Newport Jazz Festival."

The band returned to the Newport Jazz Festival the following June 29th of 1975.

The program that night included Buddy Rich and his Big Band. The program was called "Trumpet and the Drum."

Corky again returned to play "Caravan."

Audio from that concert once again showed Harry and the band to be playing up to the venue's history.

In the mid-1970s, several "audiophile" record labels began to produce "Direct to disc" vinyl albums. Labels such as "Direct Disk Labs," "Century," and "American Gramophone Co" began to record Big Band records.

Les Brown, Buddy Rich, Woody Herman and Tommy Newsome from the Tonight Show band, all were recorded using the "Direct to disc" technology.

The technology wasn't new. It was merely an upgraded version of the "old school" method of recording onto vinyl, as opposed to the shellac that was used for the first half of the twentieth century.

"Sheffield Lab" was another "audiophile" label that had tried to find a market as early as 1968.

In March of 1976, Lincoln Mayorga from Sheffield Lab approached Harry James with the idea of recording an album. The context would be that the Harry James Orchestra would play 15-20-minute sets without a break. The recording would take place in the Wylie Chapel of the First Presbyterian Church of Hollywood.

Using one single microphone, the hopes were in creating the sound that a dancer may hear while dancing to the James band live. The technology was not foolproof. The first recording sessions had to be scrapped because the recording process failed to capture the true brilliance of the Harry James trumpet sound.

The Harry James Orchestra returned to the Wylie Chapel to record again in July of 1976.

According to all who were present, everything clicked. Harry sounded great, the band sounded great, and the album "King James Version" was released in the Fall of 1976.

The brilliant pianist Tommy Todd had joined the band to replace Jack Perciful. Todd had been the pianist for the James band during the early 1950s. Todd was an excellent arranger and had written extensively for several Big Bands during the 1940s, many Hollywood movie soundtracks, and recorded with his own small groups.

Todd was also a member of the group led by Lionel Hampton for the famed "Just Jazz" concerts in 1947.

Dave Stone joined the band on bass, a position held by his father Bob Stone in the early 1950s.

The trumpet section was comprised of the ever-present Nick Buono, Bob Berrenson, Bill Hicks, and Gino Bozzacco.

Trombones were Chuck Anderson (whom Harry called his little Dixieland player), Tom Padveen, and Houghton Peterson.

Mel Kunkle had replaced Corky Corcoran in 1974, veteran lead alto Quinn Davis had been a member of the Stan Kenton and Buddy Rich bands. Pat Longo, Norm Smith, and Chuck Lawson filled out the sax section.

Our friend Bill Hicks was part of the trumpet section on the Sheffield Lab sessions. He shared his thoughts with me about the recording:

"I had been on the band a few months when we recorded "The King James Version." We recorded two 3-hour sessions a day for five days. I noticed Harry wasn't playing the same solos I had heard him play every night. He would play a new solo. Then on each subsequent take, he would make some changes or throw out that solo and play something completely different.

On the next job after the sessions, when we played one of the songs we had recorded, Harry is playing a new solo, not the same one I had heard every night before the recording sessions. He continues playing those same new solos every night. When the album comes out a few months later, I put it on the turntable, and those "new solos" are the ones that made it onto the record."

Les DeMerle was the drummer and had the distinction of being the drummer on all three of the Sheffield Lab albums.

The Sheffield Lab sessions produced enough music for two complete albums. The second album, released in 1977, was called "Comin' From a Good Place." The albums allowed Harry to record some of his favorite arrangements.

Rob Turk's beautiful arrangement of "Traces" was recorded in the Readers Digest sessions.

Dave Matthews had written for the 1939-40 Harry James Orchestra. Matthews recorded an interesting version of "Lara's Theme-Somewhere My Love." The chart had very little in common with the popular waltz from" Dr. Zhivago."

Longtime James pianist arranged "Watch What Happens" for the band in 1970. It was a staple in most of the James band performances for the remainder of Harry's life.

The Thad Jones composition "More Splutie Please," finally made its way onto a record, after having been in the James book since 1963.

(To this day, no one truly knows the definition of the word "Splutie!)

The "King James Version" went on to sell 80,000 copies. That was an amazing amount of record sales for a Big Band in the 1970s.

Harry James had the distinction of having all three of his Sheffield Lab albums nominated for a Grammy Award.

A follow-up album resulting from the Sheffield Lab sessions was called "Comin' From a Good Place."

The 1952 album "Hollywood's Best" featured Harry James and Rosemary Clooney combining to record "You'll Never Know."

"You'll Never Know" won an Academy Award for best song from a motion picture in 1943. The song written by Harry Warren and the lyrics by Mack Gordon was sung by Alice Faye in the movie "Hello Frisco Hello."

The song struck a chord in Harry James. He searched as far back as 1943 to find a version that he could play with his band. He had recorded it with a small combo in 1946.

When the collaboration with Rosemary Clooney became popular, Harry played it with the band for a couple of years.

Bob Friedlander was a musician and arranger from South Florida, although he had written for Ralph Flanagan's Orchestra and several local bands in the Miami area.

He had been trying to submit arrangements to Harry James for several years, with no results. In 1974 when the Harry James Orchestra was doing one of its Southern tours, Friedlander approached Harry James and asked if he could write an arrangement of "You'll Never Know."

Bob Friedlander wrote the arrangement that featured Harry's trumpet and a tenor sax solo (with Corky Corcoran in mind no doubt).

James knew right away that this was the version of "You'll Never Know" for which he had been searching.

The arrangement immediately became featured in most of the performances by Harry James from 1975 on.

Another chart from the "Comin' From a Good Place" album was an Ernie Wilkins composition called "The Footstomper."

Harry used to take pleasure in assuming the drum chair and playing drums on "The Footstomper" occasionally. (I saw him do it in 1979).

March 29, 1976, saw a reunion, of sorts, of Harry James and his Orchestra and his former "boy singer."

An ambitious television project called "John Denver and Friend," with said friend being Frank Sinatra, was filmed in Hollywood.

Part of the program would have Sinatra sing while accompanied by his "friends" Nelson Riddle, Count Basie and Harry James.

The James band played "Two O' Clock Jump." Then Harry accompanied Sinatra on an abbreviated rendition of "All or Nothing at All."

In October of 1976, Harry and the band appeared on a television show hosted by Peter Marshall. Marshall. Marshall had been a singer on Broadway and a band singer of sorts.

The Harry James Orchestra accompanied Marshall on "A Sinner Kissed An Angel."

Around this time, Harry James and his Orchestra were appearing at the Westbury Music Fair, with Tony Bennett, and Sarah Vaughn. The three of them appeared on the Mike Douglas Show.

Douglas joined Bennett, Vaughn, and James in a rendition of "It Don't Mean a Thing if it Ain't Got That Swing."

While the three vocalists engaged in a little scat singing, Harry James showed that his Jazz chops were still intact.

In 1977 former Freddy Martin vocalist and talk show pioneer, presented several Big Bands on his show. He continued to have the Big Band leaders and their most famous vocalists appear for the next four years.

On November 8, 1977, Griffin featured an entire broadcast with Harry James and his Orchestra, Helen Forrest, and Dick Haymes as the only guests. The program was filmed at Caesars Palace in Las Vegas.

The program enabled us to see three of the giants from the Big Band Era still performing beautifully.

The program began with Merv Griffin explaining to the audience what they were about to witness and hear. When Harry James was introduced, the audience exploded in approval.

As the curtains opened, Harry and the band played "Ciribiribin," and "Don't Be That Way."

Harry and Merv then engaged in some banter about the current status of the Big Bands.

Harry used to love to quote the saying that was attributed to both Duke Ellington and Louis Armstrong. He quoted it twice during this Griffin show broadcast:

"There's only two kinds of music. If you like it, it's good. If you don't like it, it's bad!"

Harry then changed the opening to his new arrangement of "You'll Never Know."

Rather than the ensemble playing the melody, Harry started it much the way he started his 1952 recording, with his trumpet playing the melody. Mel Kunkle played a tenor solo. Then Harry proved again that he was one of the supreme balladeers in Jazz history.

Former James vocalist Dick Haymes comes out and sings two of his recorded songs with Harry, "A Sinner Kissed An Angel," and "I'll Get By."

Haymes was enjoying a renaissance in his career. His voice was still in great shape, and it was obvious that he took pleasure in recreating his past hits with the James band.

No musical combination in all music history produced as many hit recordings as did the pairing of Harry James and Helen Forrest.

Helen returns to sing what we James fans refer to as the "Hits Medley" with the Harry James Orchestra.

Although Harry played that medley hundreds of times over the years, an interesting change occurs on the last note of the medley.

Harry always went up to a high D on the last note, as the female vocalist always came down to an F. However, on this occasion, Harry comes down to a high A, as Helen ends on a high C.

No doubt, Harry adjusted his ending to honor his dear friend and most successful "Girl Singer."

"The Sheik of Araby" begins with an intro by the wonderful Tommy Todd on piano.

Harry plays the lead in a frontline of sorts, Dixieland style. Todd plays an extended solo, followed by a trombone solo by Chuck Anderson.

Then Harry plays his solo, followed by the ensemble and Harry taking four-bar breaks.

Harry plays "Blues Stay Away from Me," showing his allegiance to Louis Armstrong.

The program closes with the obligatory "Two O' Clock Jump."

All in all, the program continues to be a historical document of the impact that Harry James had on American popular culture.

Harry James and his Orchestra returned to the Merv Griffin Show three more times over the next three and half years.

In 1978, Harry James was the opening act on an entire week of broadcasts of the Merv Griffin Show.

One particular highlight was the pairing of Harry James and trumpeter Jack Sheldon in support of Merv Griffin singing "Somebody Done Somebody Wrong Song."

I received an email a few years ago from Jack Sheldon, asking if I had the video footage of that duet.

I sent it to Jack, and he said it was one of the high points of his career, as, like me, he grew up idolizing Harry James.

Mike Butera had replaced Mel Kunkle as a tenor sax soloist with the James band. He is featured, along with Harry, on "You'll Never Know."

The James band returned to the Merv Griffin Show in 1980 and 1981.

In July of 1978, George Wein again invited Harry James to the Newport Jazz Festival. Along with the James band, the entire day, July 2, 1978, was dedicated to Big Bands. The bands of Woody Herman, Count Basie, Stan Kenton, and Buddy Rich were all featured on the day-long program.

Harry James and his Orchestra were the "surprise guests" at the festival.

The whole James band was on fire, driven by the great Sonny Payne. Although, Payne fell victim to what many believe was an orchestrated prank by Buddy Rich.

Tenor sax player Mike Butera was in the band that day. He related this story to me recently:

"But what happened when we went on, I'll NEVER FORGET. The Buddy Rich Big Band just finished their set, Buddy's band was quickly tearing down as the house band played. We got set up. The curtains open. The huge audience applause and hoots rang out as the "Surprise Big Band" was Harry James!

After the opener that only lasted 30 seconds, we immediately begin an up-tempo tune called "Apples" that featured the great Sonny Payne on a long drum solo. Now Sonny, having been Basie's drummer and Frank Sinatra's favorite drummer, was a legend. And of course, before Buddy Rich went out on his own, he had been Harry's featured drummer and the highest-paid sideman at the time.

Sonny and Buddy did not like each other. They had a major ego conflict for years. Stories would get out on the big-band gossip circuit about buddy saying harsh things about Sonny and vice versa. They hated each other even though if they met publicly. They would be friendly. Well, as Harry kicked off the tune, something felt wrong. That loud snare drum of Sonny's was not accenting the percussive phrases of the arrangement. (Sonny was the loudest drummer I have ever played with!) I looked up a Harry, and he was glaring at Sonny. After several measures, the band whimpered to a halt like a car out of gas. Sonny stood up on his drum stand and held up his snare drum to show the audience that his drumhead had been slit with a knife!

Well, I hear applause start up again, and here comes Buddy with a smile on his face, carrying his snare drum to hand it to Sonny to play!

We all felt Sonny's pain as we finished that set that day. And on the tour bus for the next few weeks, we listened to Sonny's lament: "that damn Buddy, I know he did it."

Mike Butera is now the Pastor of River City Calvary Chapel of Sacramento. He is a wonderful Bible teacher.

Still Harry After All These Years

As the James band was preparing for their Southern tour in January of 1979, Sonny Payne got very sick. He was admitted to a Los Angeles hospital with pneumonia.

Sonny had no insurance and no money with which to pay for medical treatment. Harry James agreed to pay for his treatment.

Sonny Payne died on January 29, 1979, at the age of 52.

Harry James paid for his funeral costs.

Les DeMerle stepped in to play drums for the upcoming tour.

Sheffield Lab asked Harry to record another album. They felt that they had upgraded their recording process and were confident that there would not be a repeat of the problems they had in 1976.

Harry and the band returned to the Wylie Chapel on March 26, 1979.

Over four days, they recorded "Still Harry After All These Years."

The band personnel had changed. In addition to Les DeMerle on drums, Dave Stone returned as the bass player. The regular bass player, Ira Westley, played tuba on the album.

Ira Westley was a much-beloved musician in Los Angeles. He became well known as the tuba player for the Oompah Boys on The Man Show in 1999.

Nick Buono and Bill Hicks were still in the trumpet section.

They were joined by Clay Jenkins and veteran lead trumpet player Clyde Reasinger.

Reasinger had formerly been with the Stan Kenton, Sam Donahue, Maynard Ferguson, and Quincy Jones Big Bands.

Clyde Reasinger had also played lead trumpet on the Miles Davis/Gil Evans collaborations in 1959.

In addition to Mike Butera on tenor sax, veteran alto sax player Tino Isgro, Chris Galuman on alto, the ever-present Norm Smith on tenor, and Jack Aiken filled out the sax section.

The trombones were Gary Tole, John Cochrane, and Stu Undem.

Former Kenton pianist Norm Parker had only recently replaced Tommy Todd.

Like the other two Sheffield Lab albums, Harry and the band played the tunes for side one all at once; there was no break between tunes. If someone made a mistake or kicked over a mute, they played the whole side again.

The opening tune on the album was Johnny Watson's arrangement of Juan Tizol's "Caravan." Watson had been writing for Big Bands since the 1940s. Watson wrote the chart for Harry in 1971.

Harry's playing on this tune was remarkable. His sound was pure, clean, and exhibited his command of all the registers of the trumpet.

(I own the actual arrangement used on this album. Harry's part has several sections where Harry scratched out measures and penciled in changes that he wanted to make. Especially interesting is the last solo, which he wrote in pencil on his part!)

Bob Florence's great arrangement of "Satin Doll," which had been a staple in the James book for nearly twenty years, was changed to give the melody to the bass trombone of Stu Undem.

Harry had recently added Ray Conniff's rewrite of the Benny Goodman arrangement of "Roll 'Em" to the library. On the recording, he left out his solo and chose to play the lead on the trumpet section rewrite of his original solo.

Jack Perciful's gorgeous arrangement of "Moonglow" really deserved to be recorded. Not only does it show Harry's unique usage of the low register of his horn, but the brass and sax section writing were masterful. Jack Perciful might have had a different career path, had he not joined the Harry James Orchestra in 1958.

Harry selected two throwaway tunes to include in the album. "Dance, "and "The theme from Sanford and Son." Other than being a nod to the then-new "Disco" craze, in performance, the tunes allowed Harry James to show off his cowbell skills. (This was twenty-one years before Christopher Walken popularized the cowbell on Saturday Night Live).

Time restraints caused Harry to shorten "Take the A' Train," leaving out his solo spot, in addition to the spot where Mike Butera would have played a tenor solo. The same goes for "Help Me Make It Through the Night." Jack Perciful wrote "Night" as a vocal chart, with Harry opening with a solo, then followed by a vocal. (My wife Cheryl Morris sang this with Harry often). Stu Undem plays a bass trombone solo.

The Ernie Wilkins chart on "Undecided" is taken at a comparatively laid-back tempo, showing off the precision of the James brass section.

Perhaps the high point of "Still Harry After All These Years" is the Latin-tinged ballad "Ciao."

"Ciao" is the result of something that Harry heard during the band's tour of South America in 1978. He told the story that he "caught the flavor" of a Brazilian melody. He then assigned Rob Turk to write an arrangement for "Ciao." Harry even went so far as to ask his old friend lyricist Sammy Cahn to write a set of lyrics for the tune. Evidently, Cahn wrote something, because if you research the song, it lists the co-writers as "James-Turk-Cahn."

Once again, the Harry James Orchestra was nominated for a Grammy for the album "Still Harry After All These Years."

During this time, Harry James employed a couple of different drummers.

Tony Bennett's drummer Joe Cocuzzo fulfilled a midwestern tour with the James band. Cocuzzo was a fine drummer, but certainly not a Big Band Swing drummer.

I saw the band two nights of the tour in September of 1979.

Harry and the band played a dance date at the Coliseum Ballroom in Benld, Illinois.

Joe Cocuzzo played drums on the first set. I watched Harry, and he was showing signs of unrest on his face. During the first set, the band played Ray Conniff's chart on "September Song." The first chorus of "September Song" is played by the trombone section. Chuck Anderson was playing trombone, but for some reason, the trombones weren't phrasing the way Harry wanted. He walked over behind the trombones and began playing the lead part.

He wasn't mean or bossy about it. He was acting as a teacher.

At the end of the first set, Harry pulled Joe Cocuzzo over to the side and began talking and gesturing to him.

When the band returned to the stand, they had a new drummer, Harry James!

Harry called up "The Footstomper" and played flawless, swinging drums. It was obvious that Harry could have been a legitimate Big Band drummer.

All while Harry was playing drums, Joe Cocuzzo stood off to the side and watched intently. It was obvious that Harry was teaching him what he wanted.

At the end of the tune, Cocuzzo walked to the front of his drum set, leaned down to grab the rug that his drums were sitting on, and pulled the drums about five feet forward.

When he sat back down at his drums, and the band began to play the next tune, you could see that Cocuzzo had learned what Harry was trying to teach him.

He played like a different drummer.

During the summer of 1979, American theater impresario Lee Guber and his partner Shelly Gross conceived the idea of bringing 1940s radio to life on the stage. Guber planned to take a troupe of entertainers connected to the forties, on the road as a stage show.

In 1944, no Big Band was more well known, or more successful than Harry James and his Orchestra.

Guber decided to use the James band as the centerpiece of the show. He then began to build a troupe around Harry James.

The original cast of "The Big Broadcast of 1944," was Dick Haymes, Helen Forrest, The Ink Spots. Hildegarde, and former Jack Benny sidekick Don Wilson. Wilson would serve as the on-stage "Announcer," and each of the cast would do a set of their hits, with Harry James and his Orchestra accompanying them.

The band drummer for the first shows was former Count Basie drummer Harold Jones.

My wife Cheryl Morris was the James band vocalist at that time. The producers of "The Big Broadcast of 1944," refused to write her into the show. However, at the insistence of Harry, Cheryl was featured in a "dream sequence" during the show. She also was permitted, thanks to Harry James, to join the entire ensemble for the big finish of the show, with everybody singing "God Bless America."

The show opened at the Fisher Theater in Detroit in October. This was followed by shows at the Westbury Music Theater in New York, the Valley Forge Music Fair, the Schubert Theater, and several other venues. Over the next eighteen months, the cast would change. Fran Warren,

Dennis Day, Gordon McRae, and the Pied Pipers all would serve in the cast at various times.

Dick Haymes died of lung cancer in March of 1980.

Although the show opened to good attendance, and good reviews, the logistics of keeping a troupe of that stature intact was not easy.

Guber and Gross had envisioned taking the "Big Broadcast of 1944" to Broadway.

Alas, the concept fell upon itself, and by mid-1981, everyone involved lost interest, especially the managers at prospective venues.

Harry James had grown tired of performing in New York and felt that the show conflicted with his band's normal tours.

Those of us who saw Harry James during this period could see that something was wrong with him. Of course, nobody knew that there was a serious health problem with him

He had truly lost his fire, his motivation to play. For him, it was all about standing on the stage with his band and entertaining people.

He still played well, he never played badly, but he just wasn't the same player.

In the spring of 1980, Peter Allen had written a song for Bernadette Peters' debut album. Rather than have a heavily orchestrated arrangement for the song "I Never Thought I'd Break, he decided to support Peters' vocal with a rhythm section, with him playing the piano.

The idea came that Bernadette Peters needed something special to accompany her plaintive vocal.

That something special was the golden trumpet of Harry James!

The feel of the recording was that of a Cabaret singer performing in a small club. At approximately 1:40 seconds into the song, Harry James begins playing softly behind Peters's vocal.

It is as emotive and tender performance as Harry James ever recorded. His trumpet unmistakable, and his musical sense unabated.

It is quite sad, in retrospect, that Harry James was not included in the recording of "You'll Never Know" on the Bernadette Peters album. He certainly could have added some depth to an otherwise unremarkable rendering of Harry Warren and Mack Gordon's classic ballad.

Closing the curtain

South America had become a regular tour destination for Harry James and his Orchestra by the 1970s.

March of 1981 had Harry and the band, once again heading South of the border.

Harry assembled an "all-star" band for the trip to South America.

Jack Perciful returned to the band as a pianist.

Bassist Ira Westley and Les DeMerle on drums filled out the rhythm section.

The legendary Chuck Gentry had returned to the baritone sax chair that he first held in 1940. He was joined in the sax section by Quinn Davis on lead alto, Ed Easton, and Norm Smith on tenor. John Keeling was the second alto sax.

Chuck Anderson, Michael Millar, and Steven Tyler were on trombone.

The trumpet section had Lin Biviano, Bill Barrett, and Hal Espinosa, joining Nick Buono.

Veteran Big Band singer Lynn Roberts had joined the band after Cheryl Morris had left the band.

The band returned to Disneyland to perform in the Carnation Plaza on September 1, 1981.

When Carnation Plaza first opened in 1956, it became a place where many of the top Big Bands could appear regularly. In 1984, Peter Marshall hosted a cable television series called "Big Bands at Disneyland." Marshall would introduce the bandleader, and the band would play, then Marshall would interview with the famous bandleaders.

Harry James had been a regular at the Carnation Plaza since 1961.

My wife Cheryl Morris joined the band for a week of performances at Disneyland. Audio recordings of the performances showed Harry to be still playing well. He played his regular sets and even played "Ultra" on at least one occasion. He didn't attempt to play the high notes in his solo but still managed to play up to a high D with authority.

Pictures from the appearance showed that Harry had lost considerable weight. He didn't appear as the imposing figure that he always had. His voice was softer, and a little hoarse when he announced Cheryl or the soloists.

True to form, Harry kept the band playing, especially on the road. The last two years of Harry's life found him doing what he loved doing, playing his trumpet, and entertaining his fans.

My friend Tony Crapis played lead trumpet on the James band for most of the last two years. He shared with me how the tours often started:

"Nick Buono, Harry, and I would always fly out together. Sometimes Eddie Easton would fly down from reno and meet us in Vegas to all fly out together. We had great times at the airport bars in Vegas and other airports waiting for our flight to go. The others who would fly with us were Gino Bozzacco and Joey Singer.

Joey would room with me on a few tours until I got my own room. Lots of great memories. I also have quite a few cassette tapes of the band during concerts that we did. I was happy, sad, and honored to be his last Lead Trumpet player the last two years he was alive."

The itineraries from the last two years of Harry's life were, as usual, filled with one-nighters. Some of the venues where Harry had been playing for decades, were on the calendar for his final tours.

Folks that saw and heard the band during that time have told me that he still played great. He was still Harry James!

By early 1982, it became apparent to everyone that Harry was sick. No one knew the extent or nature of his illness. It was during this time that Harry complained about pain in his throat and neck. A cursory exam suggested that the problems stemmed from Harry's dental implants, which had been a source of aggravation for nearly twenty years.

They removed his implants and gave him dentures. The dentures seemed to hasten the decline of his playing.

On February 24, 1982, Harry was asked to be co-presenter of the Grammy Award for Best Jazz Vocal Performance. The award went to Al Jarreau. It was surreal to see Harry James and Chuck Mangione appear on television.

Harry looked much older than his sixty-six years. Yet his spirits and sense of humor seemed intact.

Harry and Me one last time

I was performing in a combo at a small club in Denver in early April of 1983. A patron came in one night and slapped a copy of the National Enquirer on the bar.

He said to me, "Your buddy isn't doing so good!"

The headline said, "Harry James Fighting Cancer."

I stared at the paper in disbelief. It didn't seem possible.

The next morning, I called my friend Viola Monte at the Harry James office in California. I asked her if it were true, but Vi said that they thought Harry was going to pull through.

Harry had a cancerous tumor removed from his neck on April 4th. The doctor told the Montes that Harry only had three months to live.

Harry continued to work as much as he could. On April 15th, Harry fulfilled an agreement to record some solos for an album featuring Japanese actress and singer Kei Miramura. The label was "Discomate," a Japanese label.

Nelson Riddle was the arranger, although few people believe that Riddle wrote the charts himself. The tracks were recorded in Japan, and Harry went into the studio to solo on three tracks.

Harry was very weak, yet he gave it his best. The solos were tentative, but the sound of Harry James was unmistakable.

The agreement that the Monte's had made with Riddle and the Discomate label was that the album could never be released in the United States.

Frank Monte was very protective of Harry's public persona. He intended to keep people from seeing Harry in such a bad condition.

The doctors scheduled a regimen of chemotherapy for Harry. However, he stopped taking them.

Harry was resigned to his fate.

He continued to ask Montes to let him perform. Again, because he was so sick, and their protectiveness of his legacy, they kept telling him no.

In May of 1983, I received an itinerary from Viola Monte. Harry and the band were going to play two dates in Denver, where I was living then.

I bought tickets to see Harry at the Holiday Inn-Holidome East of Denver on June 10th.

When we walked through the front door of the venue, there was a giant "Get Well" card in the lobby, where the local radio station KEZW announcers were encouraging all the attendees to sign for Harry.

We walked to a table and chose our seats. My eyes immediately began searching for Harry James.

I was not prepared for what I saw.

Seated at a two-top table behind the stage, was Harry and his lady friend. He looked almost unrecognizable.

I approached his table and said, "Hi, Mr. James." (I was 29 years old, but I had never called him anything but "Mr. James.)

He looked up at me, not trying to stand. He extended his very small hand and said, "Hi, Kid!"

I truly was fighting back the tears, not knowing what to say.

I told him, "Mr. James, I just want you to know how much you mean to me and how much I owe you."

"I love you!"

He looked up at me, extended his hand again, and replied, "I love you too Kid!"

I found my way back to my table. I had smuggled in a small tape recorder and recorded the first set the band played.

Tino Isgro, the lead alto player, counted off "The Mole."

It was a very good band. Hal Espinosa was on lead trumpet; Nick Buono was in his customary chair.

Ed Easton was playing tenor, and Chuck Gentry was playing baritone. The lead trombone player was the wonderful Bob Havens, who was with Lawrence Welk for decades. Michael Millar was also on trombone.

Gregg Field, who was Basie's last drummer, and Frank Sinatra's last drummer, would be Harry James's last drummer.

At the end of "The Mole," the KEZW announcer spoke into the microphone.

"Isn't that a great band?"

He followed with "Ladies and Gentlemen...HARRY JAMES!"

Harry slowly made it to the stage. There was no "Ciribiribin."

In a very hoarse voice, Harry said, "Are you ready to swing? Let's Go!"

Harry counted off "Don't Be That Way" in a perfect Swing tempo. The band was truly in a groove, perhaps feeling the importance of the occasion.

Harry was leaning with his back against the piano when he began his solo.

It was apparent that Harry had little strength to play his trumpet. However, it was also clear that his musical mind was still functioning as well as ever.

He knew the limitations dealt him by his illness. The notes he played were right, staying in the middle register, which was all the range he had left.

He knew what he could play and what he couldn't.

"Tuxedo Junction" followed with Harry playing the familiar muted trumpet phrase.

Harry introduced his vocalist Stephanie Caravella who sang "Embraceable You, also featuring a tenor solo by Ed Easton.

Ed Easton was next featured on the theme from the "Pink Panther."

The fine arrangement of "Opus One" with a muted solo by Harry, was the next tune.

Harry announced a short break. He then went backstage, where Sal Monte enabled Harry to put on an oxygen mask.

During the next set, Harry told the audience, "Healthy people can't breathe in this town, and look where my clever Manager books me!"

The wonderful Chuck Gentry played the baritone sax solo on "Sweet Georgia Brown."

Harry announced the "Two O' Clock Jump." He played the opening solo but was not able to play the customary triplets with the trumpet section, nor his usual solos to close the arrangement.

Harry came out for the third set to play the "Harry James Hits Medley" with Stephanie Caravella. It was the best playing Harry did all night. As he played the familiar songs in the medley, I realized that it would be the last time I would hear Harry James play.

As he announced another break, he asked the audience, "Have you ever tried Grand Marnier and hot tea? Try it; it'll help!"

Sal Monte met Harry as he walked off the stage. Sal led him back to the oxygen tank.

That was the last time I saw Harry James.

The band played a dance at the Cherry Creek Country Club in Denver the next night. However, I decided not to attend.

On June 26th, Harry played his last engagement at the Century Plaza in Los Angeles.

Hal Espinosa, who was the lead trumpet player for the last three performances by Harry, described that last gig to me:

"The one gig that stands out for me was his last gig at Century Plaza Hotel in Los Angeles. As you know, Harry was very sick. He missed a job in Bakersfield, where Ray Anthony showed up in his place because Harry was in the hospital for treatment.

A short time later, we were playing that job at the Century Plaza with Harry out in front of the band. We were playing to a large crowd, so the ballroom was opened up to its full capacity. So, the Hotel had a camera recording the band. It was being used to project the image of the band to the crowd on either end of the ballroom.

At that time, I was a Trustee on the Local 47's Executive Board, and Pee Wee knew it, so he made sure that the recording was destroyed after the job ended. It was very unfortunate because Harry played great, sounded better than ever, didn't crack a note, and seemed to have gotten his life back. He sounded like his old self.

A few days later, maybe a week or two, I was awakened by a phone call from a local radio station informing me that Harry had died and wanted an interview. I was shocked! He was my idol since I was a kid, and now he was dead."

On July 5, 1983, I turned on the radio to hear the news. The lead story was that Harry James had died at 67 years old.

I had been expecting that news for several days. But it still was traumatic.

Several news and radio stations played tributes to Harry James that day, all across the country.

Of all the musicians that I had ever seen or heard, Harry James truly invincible. He had remained so consistent, at such a high level of performing, that the end seemed so very fast.

To this day, the trumpet Harry James remains the most identifiable sound of all trumpet players, except for Harry's idol Louis Armstrong.

So many of Harry's friends and fellow musicians attended his memorial service. Frank Sinatra gave the eulogy.

People still visit his crypt at Bunkers Eden Vale Memorial Park in Las Vegas.

I was able to be photographed at his star on the Hollywood Walk of Fame several years ago.

The impact of Harry James on me cannot be measured. His sound was the sound that I wanted.

But that is impossible because Harry James was born with that sound in his soul.

Life after Harry

In the Fall of 1983, about three months after the death of Harry James, a meeting was convened.

Frank, Sal, and Viola Monte called a meeting of select members of the Harry James Orchestra.

Among the members present were Cheryl Morris, Clyde Reasinger, Ira Westley, and a few others.

Frank Monte announced to all present that it was time to decide the future of the band. A new leader needed to be selected.

Sometime between the time when Harry James was admitted to Valley Hospital in Las Vegas, and July 5 when Harry died, Harry and Frank "Pee Wee" Monte discussed the future of the band.

According to Monte, Harry had told him that he wanted the band to continue without him. It is not known whether Harry suggested a new leader, but when Pee Wee Monte gathered his select group, he had a list.

(I had thrown my hat in the ring to lead the James band at this time. But Frank Monte insisted that he wanted a "Name" trumpet player.)

My wife, Cheryl Morris, was a unanimous choice to be the band vocalist. Her memories of the event were that the group of Harry James Orchestra members sat and listened to records of prospective leaders.

According to some, British trumpet star Kenny Baker was suggested. In hindsight, he would have been a great choice, because his approach to soloing with a Big Band was similar to Harry's. However, logistically Baker's selection was impossible because he lived in England.

As Frank Monte played a few selections from the "Time-Life" recordset, a name continued to emerge.

Many of Harry's solos had been recreated on those records, and most were played by trumpet player Joe Graves.

Joe Graves was a highly respected trumpet player who had played in the trumpet sections of bands led by Bob Crosby, Ray McKinley, Jimmy Dorsey, and Charlie Barnet. He became part of the Capitol Records' all-star stable of great musicians in the 1950s. He was eventually called upon to record the solos of Bunny Berigan, Charlie Spivak, Billy Butterfield, and Harry James, among others.

The assembled members of Harry's band agreed that, if he was willing and able, Joe Graves could come closest to recreating Harry's classic solos.

Over a series of meetings, another former James band veteran in attendance at the first meeting was the wonderful arranger Jack Mathias. Pee Wee wanted Mathias to rewrite many of Harry James' greatest hits, without strings.

It had always been a source of conflict between Monte and his famous bandleader star, that Harry refused to dwell in the past. He did not want to play most of his best-selling songs.

Joe Graves accepted the offer to lead the Harry James Orchestra. However, it became obvious that Graves was not the same trumpet player from all those great records from the fifties and sixties.

Also, Joe Graves was having some serious dental issues.

Joe was not an accomplished frontman. He was rather introverted and not a showman. But he was a very nice man, and everybody loved him.

The band began performing as the "Harry James Orchestra under the direction of Joe Graves" in January of 1984. For the next four years, the band continued to work and tour regularly.

Joe Graves did a respectable job playing Harry's parts, though he was not a real jazz improviser. Most of the great Jazz charts that Harry had commissioned over the years were not played much.

In 1985, PBS decided to film a "Tribute to Harry James" for a television special. Billy Taylor was selected as the emcee, and Helen Forrest came to sing some of her famous hits. It was filmed during a dance engagement at the famed Peony Park Ballroom in Omaha, Nebraska.

Cheryl Morris was singing on that date, but her vocals were edited out of the finished product. Helen Forrest sang HER versions of the hits she recorded with Harry James.

Chuck Gentry was featured as the baritone sax soloist on "Sweet Georgia Brown." Joe Graves recreated Harry's solos on several tunes, including "Sleepy Lagoon" and "Just a Gigolo."

In retrospect, it was a poorly edited, low budget production from PBS.

The memory of Harry James deserved better!

By late 1987, Joe Graves' dental issues had reached a crisis point. It was obvious that he could no longer front the Harry James Orchestra.

Former Harry James lead trumpet player, Art Depew, took over the leadership position for the James band. Depew was well known in the California music scene, after being a member of the Lawrence Welk band in the 1950s.

Depew's trumpet playing skills were still intact, and he was able to recreate many of the famous James hits.

Art Depew was able to get the Harry James Orchestra in a recording studio in 1994. The James band was selected to accompany Barry Manilow on the James/Sinatra arrangement of "All or Nothing at All." The album was the first Barry Manilow album to become a gold record since his 1990 Christmas album.

"The Harry James Orchestra under the direction of Art Depew" recorded an album for Wally Heider's Hindsight Records label in 1997. The album was called "The Harry James Orchestra Live at the Palladium." The vocalist on the album was Cassie Miller.

Art Depew stepped down permanently from the leadership of the Harry James Orchestra in 1998.

In retrospect, both Graves and Depew continued the tradition of the Harry James Orchestra with great respect and with moderate success.

In 1998, the James estate Fred Radke, who had been in the James trumpet section briefly in 1969, to lead the band.

Singer Cheryl Morris left the Harry James Orchestra in early 1990. She moved to Portland, Oregon, shortly after to raise her young son.

In 2009, I joined a Facebook group called the "Harry James Appreciation Society."

One day, a lady named Cheryl Monteiro joined the Facebook group. She posted that she was a former singer with Harry James, and if anyone ever cared to discuss her days as Harry's girl singer, she would be glad to chat with them.

I sent her a message saying, "I know you! I saw you with Harry in St, Louis in 1979!"

Once she determined that I wasn't a stalker, we began texting regularly. I was in Northeast Ohio, and she was in Portland, Oregon.

For the next six months, we began chatting every day and then talking on the phone.

On September 1, 2009, I packed a suitcase and went to Portland to visit Cheryl.

On the fifth day that I was there, Cheryl was singing with a band at a church dance. The band let me sing and play a couple of tunes.

That night I asked Cheryl to marry me. We got married on October 20, 2009.

When Cheryl called our Friend Viola Monte and told her that she had married Chuck Par-Due, Viola squealed into the phone, "You married our little Chuckie!"

And it was all because of God's grace, and our relationship with the World's Greatest Trumpet player.

Thank you, Harry!

We miss you every day.

Harry and Me-1970

My Dad's name was Chuck Par-Due I. I am Chuck II. The "second."

Dad named me a "second" because he thought the name "Junior" was demeaning.

My Dad was a very talented musician and vocalist, who led small bands in the West Virginia area during the 1940s.

Although he was well known locally, he never received much attention outside of his environs.

There was one exception.

In 1946, an unscrupulous booking agent sold the story of my parents' courtship to Twentieth Century Fox. The results were a motion picture called "You Were Meant for Me," starring Dan Dailey as my Dad's character, and Jeanne Crain as my Mom.

In the movie, Dan Dailey played "Chuck Arnold" (my Dad and my middle name), a singing, dancing, saxophone player.

My Dad sang, dance expertly, and played saxophone.

In those days, lawsuits against big corporations like 20th Century Fox were unheard of, if not impossible.

In the end, my parents never received a dime for their story, which, according to my Mom, was quite accurate.

My folks tried for eight years to have a child. They even gave up and began adoption proceedings to adopt a baby boy.

Until my Mom discovered she was expecting...ME!

Four months after I was born, I got very sick. The doctor said I had croup.

It became double pneumonia, and both my lungs collapsed.

They rushed me to the hospital, where they were told that there was nothing the doctors could do.

However, there was a young Intern from Havana, Cuba, who grabbed a scalpel and cut my throat open. He inserted a tube to pump up my lungs, and the color returned to my skin.

The prognosis was not good. The doctors told my parents that I was so weak that I might not live past the age of five.

They were wrong.

At the age of nine, my Dad took me to a piano teacher. After about six weeks, the teacher told my Dad that "I didn't have it." This was a disappointment to my Dad, and his mother, who was a piano player.

In the eighth grade, I decided to be a drummer.

Into my life came Jesse Pearl.

He was my percussion instructor and Junior High band director.

He was a no-nonsense teacher, who would interrupt conversations in a class by hurling a chalked-up eraser at the head of the offender.

He never threw an eraser at me.

Mr. Pearl was one of the finest men I ever knew, and a fine musician whose specialty was the saxophone.

I survived two years of Junior High school band and began to plan my entrance into tenth grade.

I used to play Gene Krupa's records incessantly. My dream was to learn how to play Gene's solos on "Sing, Sing, Sing" with Benny Goodman.

I later realized that the reason I could not learn the piano and was a lousy drummer was that I have manual dexterity issues. I am very clumsy.

I still am!

One day, I went to the local library, and they had gotten the Columbia Record of the 1938 Benny Goodman Carnegie Hall Concert.

As I listened to the live version of "Sing, Sing, Sing," I became enraptured by the trumpet solo in the second half of the performance.

It was from Harry James. I had never heard anything like that before.

I listened to the record over and over, dropping the needle at the end of Babe Russin's sax solo.

In the Summer of 1968, I built up the nerve to proclaim to my Dad that I had decided that I wanted to be a trumpet player.

In retrospect, I had put my Dad in a difficult decision. As a musician himself, he realized that probably, I indeed "didn't have it!"

Instead, he announced that I could not play the trumpet, because the doctors said my lungs were too weak to play a wind instrument. I had severe Asthma episodes throughout my childhood.

I persisted. "Dad, I'd rather be dead than not be a trumpet player!". A very stupid pronouncement from a skinny, sickly fourteen-year-old!

He shook his head, and we dropped the discussion.

I entered the twelfth grade as a percussionist. I was too clumsy to play the snare drum, but I was efficient on the bells and the tympany.

One day in September of 1968, I was called to the school office. My Dad's best friend Grover was there to tell me that my Dad had collapsed on the floor, after having taken my three brothers and me to school.

Grover took me to the Veterans Hospital in Miami, Florida.

They operated on Dad and determined that his intestines had ruptured, and peritonitis had set in. Dad survived the surgery, was given a colostomy, and sent home.

About a week later, Dad had asked Grover to take him shopping.

I came home from school to see a trumpet case and a copy of the "Harry James Trumpet Method" on the dining room table. He had spent $100 of money he could ill-afford to spend.

Once again, Jesse Pearl entered my life.

Dad had gone to see Mr. Pearl and told him that although he doubted that I was teachable, he thought he owed it to his Son to try.

Mr. Jesse Pearl was enlisted to attempt to teach me the trumpet.

He gave it his best, but after about a month gave up.

"You are never going to be a trumpet player until you quit trying to sound like Harry James!"

(Over forty years later, Mr. Pearl told me that he was glad that he was wrong about me. Via Facebook, Mr. Pearl would encourage, and critique the sixty-year-old version of me, every time I posted a YouTube video. He did this until his death in October of 2019)

I became obsessed with the trumpet. Hurrying through my homework, to practice my trumpet for two, or three, or four hours a day.

My Dad decided to play a New Year's Eve gig on saxophone, despite being warned not to. He ruptured his colostomy and was rushed to Veterans Hospital.

That's when they found the Colon Cancer that was missed four months earlier.

It was terminal.

My Dad tried to remain strong for as long as he could.

In the Summer of 1969, Dad was lying on the makeshift bed he had made for himself. He wanted to make sure that his pain did not interrupt my Mom's sleep.

I brought him a copy of the Miami Herald. The headline on the Entertainment page was "Harry James Coming to Miami." For the first time in twenty-five years, Harry James and his Orchestra was going to appear at the Miami Springs Villas.

My Dad and I both knew that he wouldn't be around in January.

We never mentioned it again.

Chuck Par-Due went to Heaven on September 26th, 1969.

My life was turned inside out.

On January 30th, 1970, Mom kept me home from school. I asked her why, and she said she wanted to take me shopping for some new clothes. We went to JC Penney's, where she bought me a navy-blue double-breasted suit with new shoes, and a dress shirt.

Something was afoot, but I didn't know what.

Around 7:00 PM that night, the doorbell rang. I opened the door, and there was a uniformed chauffeur at the door, with a big black limousine parked at the curb.

The driver said he was there to pick up Mr. Par-Due.

Mom hurriedly explained to me that I was going to see Harry James!

I eventually found out that my Dad had called his friend Larry Birger who was the Editor of the Miami Herald. He explained to Larry that he was near death but wondered if there was any way that his kid could go to see Harry James in January.

Mr. Birger told him that he would find a way.

The limousine pulled to the front door, and the chauffeur opened the door for me.

Underarm was tucked my cheap Radio Shack cassette recorder with a couple of blank tapes

I was met at the door by a man named Art Bruns, who was the manager of the posh Miami Springs Villas. He shook my hand, treated me like royalty!

We walked into this large banquet room. My eyes immediately looked to the front of the room. There on risers were fourteen lighted band fronts. They were blue, with the initials "HJ" written in white cursive letters.

Thinking of it today still raises my heart rate!

Mr. Bruns led me to the off-stage bar area, where he took a couple of Polaroid photos of me with some of the James band members.

Then he led me to the bar, where stood Harry James.

He was dressed in a white suit, a light blue Edwardian shirt with a gold medallion fastened at the neck.

My eyes shifted to the bar, where there was a red-velour pillow, with the letters "HJ" embroidered in gold.

Resting on the pillow, was a bright golden trumpet, with a faded gold mouthpiece and the name "Harry James" engraved on the side.

Art Bruns said to Harry, "Harry, this is Chuck Par-Due."

Harry laid down his milkshake glass filled with Brandy Alexander, turned to me, and extended his right hand.

"Nice to meet you, Chuck. I've heard a lot about you".

He'd heard about me. (years later I found out what he meant).

Bruns took a Polaroid of Harry and Me. Harry signed it "To Chuck Best Wishes, Harry James" (I wish I still had that photo, long lost.

"You want a Coke kid?" said the World's Greatest Trumpet player.

Harry got me a Coke and said, "C'mon Kid," and I followed.

Harry led me to his private table upon which there were printed signs which read, "Harry James, Frank Monte, Corky Corcoran, Cathy Chemi, Tempest Storm (Harry's Date), and CHUCK PAR-DUE.

Moments later, Harry introduced to Frank "Pee Wee" Monte, his Manager.

Monte shook my hand, and nervously spied my cheap tape recorder.

"You can't record the band with that. It's against Union rules!"

Harry intervened, "Aw c'mon Frank, let the kid get his $#@&! Tape!"

Harry took my cassette recorder and placed it under Jack Perciful's piano bench.

The time came to begin the first set.

Corky Corcoran counted off the tempo for "The Mole."

I had never heard a Big Band live.

The sound was mesmerizing!

Then Harry ascended the steps up the riser and began to play the waltz version of "Ciribiribin."

I never knew a trumpet could sound that powerful. Not loud, just powerful. Harry's sound was full enough to fill the entire banquet room.

Next came, "Don't Be That Way."

The spotlights were quite bright as they shone on Harry. When he began his solo, to my sixteen-year-old eyes, it seemed as though there was steam coming out of the bell of that King trumpet.

Throughout the first set, the sound of that band, with Sonny Payne on drums, was overwhelming.

As the first set ended, Harry walked up to me and said, "Hey kid, are you hungry?"

I wasn't, but I didn't protest. Harry ordered a triple-decker ham sandwich. Harry took a section and handed the plate to me.

It had mayonnaise on it.

I hate mayonnaise!

But I shared a ham sandwich with the World's greatest trumpet player.

Moments later, a waitress approached Harry with a drink and a napkin with a request written on it.

The request came from Joe DiMaggio, a former New York Yankee star.

Harry James was a Cardinals fan.

He politely told the waitress, "You tell that SOB that if he wants to hear a song, to come to tell me himself!"

Only 32 minutes of the recording from that night remains.

As a kid, I always liked to sit up and listen to the "NEW YEAR'S EVE ALL STAR PARADE OF BANDS" on NBC Radio.

On December 31st, 1970, Harry James appeared on the Parade of Bands live from the Desert Inn in Las Vegas.

The James band was on fire that night. Vocalist Cathy Chemi was featured on "Didn't We," and the band accompanied singer Billy Daniels on "I Can't Give You Anything but Love."

Dick Spencer had just joined the band as a lead alto. He was featured on "Take the A' Train." Corky Corcoran and Harry shared the spotlight on "Cherry."

Of course, the broadcast closed with "Two O' Clock Jump." Throughout the broadcast, Sonny Payne drove the band, and Harry James was sizzling!

Harry and Me-1971-73

I received an itinerary in December 1970 for the James band's upcoming Southern tour.

Harry always liked to tour the South in January-March every year so that he could follow his St. Louis Cardinals during Spring Training in Florida.

I saw the band twice in 1971.

The Harry James Orchestra performed a concert at South Dade Senior High School in January 1971. The concert featured tunes like "Ultra" and "Malaguena Salerosa."

Again, that month, I went to see Harry at the Pier 66 Hotel in Fort Lauderdale, Florida.

The performance by Harry and the band was spectacular. He played many of the tunes that I had listened to over and over again as a teenager.

Tunes like "September Song," "Spinning Wheel," "Always," "Blue Skies," and "You Made Me Love You."

Cathy Chemi was the vocalist, and she remains, in my opinion, among the finest vocalists that Harry James ever employed.

I got to spend time when Harry before and during the dance sets. He always treated me as an equal and with respect.

The following year, 1972, Harry and the band returned to Miami. Harry once again performed at the South Dade Senior High School in Homestead, Florida.

I got to spend quite a bit of time with Harry that evening. He and the band were in rare form. In addition to many of the HJ favorites, he and the band performed a new Johnnie Watson arrangement of "Caravan."

Corky played an extended solo on "Caravan," and Harry showed off his high range and masterful technique.

The highlight of the concert was a performance of "The Sheik of Araby," from his new album "Mr. Trumpet."

Harry's solos and breaks on "Sheik" were some of the best I ever heard him play.

Back in Harry's dressing room, I asked him how I could ever get a trumpet-like his. His golden KING Harry James model was so gorgeous.

Before Harry could answer my question, his manager Frank "Pee Wee" Monte jumped in.

"Those horns are not available to the general public kid!"

I looked at Harry, and he said simply, "C'mon Frank, get the kid a trumpet!"

I didn't mention it again.

Two days later, I received a phone call from Bill Wickersham, who was the Sales Manager for KING Musical Instruments in Eastlake, Ohio.

He said that he had received a phone call from Harry James' office. He wanted to know where I wanted my Harry James model trumpet shipped.

Harry was a very kind man, especially to anyone who didn't try and take advantage of him, and those who were honest and real.

Six months later, I got my KING Harry James model trumpet.

The following February, I went to see Harry and the band at the Pompano Beach Senior High School.

The performance of Harry and the band was probably the most exciting one I ever saw live.

From the very beginning of the concert, Harry was completely on fire!

The drummer was Johnny Gillick, who is well known as a fine Dixieland drummer

In addition to "Take the A' Train," "Satin Doll," and the rest of his 1970s material, he played a poignant version of "Do You Know What It Means to Miss New Orleans." He was accompanied by only Jack Perciful on piano.

He climaxed his solo on "New Orleans," taking the last eight bars of the melody up an octave, finishing on a high F sharp. It was a powerful rendition.

After the concert, I waited outside Harry's dressing room until I got the sign from Pee Wee Monte that I could enter. I was proudly carrying my King trumpet case, containing the Harry James model trumpet that Harry had arranged for me to receive.

Harry was sitting in a chair, smoking a cigarette, enjoying his beverage of choice. When I walked into the room, Harry laid down his vices and stood to shake my hand.

He said, "Hey, Kid! What'cha got in the case?"

My hands were trembling as I sat on the floor next to Harry's chair. I opened my trumpet case and handed my new trumpet to Harry James.

The World's Greatest trumpet player took my new Harry James model, King trumpet, rocked it up and down a few times, and said, "Too damn heavy!"

It took me many years to understand why Harry James said what he said.

Like everything else in his life, he either liked something, or he didn't. He could feel a difference between his trumpet and a trumpet that was exactly like his.

Harry and Me-1979

In January of 1979, I received an itinerary from Viola Monte, detailing the band's upcoming tour. Harry and the band were going to be in West Helena, Arkansas, on February 10th.

At that time, I was living in Springfield, Missouri. Helena, Arkansas, was about a six-hour drive.

My wife (at the time) and I drove the six hours to Phillips Community College in West Helena.

We chose our seats, and I went backstage to find Harry and Pee Wee Monte. Harry was dressing for the gig.

"How you doin' Kid?"

I told Harry that I had gotten married since the last time I had seen him. I told him that, if possible, I would like for my wife to meet him.

Pee Wee told me that after the concert when it was time, he would motion for me to come backstage.

As I was walking to my seat, I heard people talking about Sonny Payne, which I thought was very odd.

As the concert began, a local radio announcer named "Sunshine" Sonny Payne came out to introduce the band.

Harry was playing very well and featured several tunes that were to be recorded in March for Sheffield Lab.

There came the point during the program when Harry began to introduce Les DeMerle for a drum feature. Harry told the audience that Sonny Payne, the drummer, was supposed to be on tour with the band. However, a few days before the band left for the tour, Sonny had gotten sick and passed away.

He then said the Les DeMerle had graciously agreed to play drums for the tour.

After the concert, as the audience filed out, I saw Pee Wee Monte stick his head out from a concert. He motioned for me to come backstage.

My wife and I walked behind the curtain, and there stood Harry. He was wearing his St. Louis Cardinal jacket.

He extended his hand to us and said it was nice to meet my wife.

She said to Harry, "It was nice to hear Sleepy Lagoon" played the right way!"

I guess that was an insult to me.

.

He signed a picture for her.

Harry was always kind and respectful to me, and that day to us.

The following August, I received another itinerary from Viola. The band was going to be on another tour and would be near St. Louis for two nights.

In September of 1979, I drove to St. Louis. My wife was expecting our first Daughter and was not interested in making the five-hour drive to see Harry.

Harry James and his Orchestra were appearing at the Plantation Dinner Theater in St. Louis, Missouri.

I walked into the lobby and found my friend, trombonist Chuck Anderson. We chatted for a few minutes and then walked into the theater.

Immediately in front of us, stood Harry, Pee Wee, and a young blonde woman.

I asked Chuck 'who the chick was.'

Chuck replied, "She's the new singer."

While I noticed that she was quite pretty, I was only interested in seeing Harry.

The band took the stage, and Harry began playing his theme.

I noticed a few changes in the personnel since I had seen the band in February.

The drummer was former Tony Bennett drummer Joe Cocuzzo.

Trumpeter Bill Hicks was also gone.

I remember that night was the only time that I ever heard Harry play the Thad Jones arrangement of "String of Pearls" live.

Harry played great that night, and the band was tight.

The next morning, I picked up Chuck Anderson, pianist Norm Parker, and one other band member in my car.

They were stuck at the motel all day, so I took them on a tour of the sights in St. Louis.

We toured the Meramec Caverns. We even sang "Ciribirbin" in four-part harmony, in an echoing cave.

We also visited "The Arch."

That night the band was playing at the famed "Coliseum Ballroom" in Benld, Illinois.

From 1924 until 2011, the "Coliseum Ballroom" featured many of the Big Bands and big-name musical acts. Names like Count Basie, Duke

Ellington, Tommy Dorsey, and Guy Lombardo appeared there. Later the Everly Brothers, Chuck Berry, and Heart performed there.

Sadly, the "Coliseum Ballroom" burned to the ground in 2011.

The atmosphere was more casual than the dinner theater show had been the previous night.

The dancers were treated to a night of great swing music, and Harry James was his usual polite, professional self as he talked to the patrons.

I got to spend a little time with Harry, both backstage and at the bar.

At one point, a local AFM Union officer approached Harry James with the intent of collecting union dues.

Harry pointed at Frank Monte and replied, "Go see that guy; he's got the checkbook!"

After the next set, Harry and I were standing at the bar when a local St. Louis radio personality name "Cactus" Charlie Menees asked Harry if he could ask him a few questions for an article about the band.

The interview went well enough until Menees asked him a question that Harry didn't like.

Charlie Menees asked Harry, "How does this group compare with groups you've led in the past?"

Harry's eyes glowed brightly as he answered, "This is a band! It's not a group; it's a BAND!"

With that, Harry downed his drink and marched to the stage.

I guess the interview was over!

I continued to notice the young singer. Not only was she very pretty, but she had an amazing voice.

She named was Cheryl Morris, and to this day, I consider her as one of the three best female singers that Harry James ever hired.

Helen Forrest, Cathy Chemi, and Cheryl Morris had the finest voices of all Harry's girl singers, in my opinion.

The funny thing was that although I heard Cheryl Morris sing those two nights, I never met her. I only got as close as six feet from her.

Harry played great that night, and he even played drums on "The Footstomper" during the second set.

At the end of the night, I got to say my goodbyes to Harry and Pee Wee.

Harry asked me, "Hey, Kid, you still got that, trumpet?"

I told him I did.

He then told me, "I'll have Vi call King and get you another one."

I got another one a few weeks later.

Viola

As I am writing this part of the book today, we are amid a Worldwide Pandemic. The medical community is battling a virus called the "Coved 19" virus. As a result, we have been in a Government-mandated "Stay at Home" situation. I have been the official "Hunter-Gatherer" for Cheryl and me. I get to go to the store to purchase needed items.

With so much time on my hands, I have been filling my days with more reading than usual, and extra time to practice my trumpet.

Yesterday, I went out into the garage in hopes of finding a specific picture. I found family pictures that I have not seen in many years. These included pictures of my Mom and Dad waiting for me to be born. Pictures of me as a baby, and as a toddler, mingled with pictures of my Children and Grandchildren.

In the middle of those pictures, I came across an envelope. It was addressed to "Mr. Chuck Par-Due 3795 West 6th Ct, Hialeah, Florida."

The postmark was missing, but I knew that it had to have been mailed in 1969-71.

The return address was from "The Harry James Orchestra, Hollywood, California."

I know that envelope had been sent from the hand of Viola Monte.

From 1943 until 2005, any envelope that originated from The Harry James Orchestra was sealed by Viola Monte.

In September of 1939, a fifteen-year-old girl named Viola Catherine Paulich went to the "World's Fair" in New York City.

The "World's Fair" featured the new Big Band led by trumpet player Harry James. He featured his young male vocalist Frank Sinatra on at least one radio broadcast emanating from the "World's Fair."

Young Viola Paulich was smitten by that trumpet player. She asked James for an autograph. Viola told him that she had started a "Harry James Fan Club" in her hometown of Kings, New York.

It wasn't long before Viola's "Harry James Fan Club" endeavors came to the attention of The Monte brothers, Fred and Frank.

In those days, Harry James needed all the fans he could get!

By August of 1943, Viola, by now eighteen, had convinced the Montes that she had acquired significant enough secretarial skills, that she could handle the ever-increasing office tasks necessitated by the huge amounts of fan mail generated by Harry's now successful music and movie ventures.

Fred Monte had been drafted, so Viola Paulich took over the secretarial tasks in the James office.

She held that job for nearly sixty-two years!

When the Harry James Orchestra office left New York City in May of 1944, Viola Paulich moved with them.

Frank "Pee Wee" Monte had completed his Army service and began booking the James band from Hollywood.

By May of 1944, Harry James was indeed a big business.

Sometime during the next few years, Viola and Frank became a couple. The seventeen-year difference never mattered to Frank and Vi.

On April 21, 1951, Frank and Viola got married.

The "Montes" were as devoted a married couple as there has ever been.

In 1958, Pee Wee Monte left the James band to manage the career of another trumpet player. Famed trumpet player and teacher Claude Gordon had formed a Big Band.

In 1959, the Claude Gordon band had been selected as the "Best Big Band of 1959."

During Frank Monte's absence, Sal Monte had taken over the leadership of the "Harry James Orchestra" business.

The Claude Gordon Orchestra proved to be an unsuccessful venture, and Frank Monte returned to the James band.

For the two and a half decades that followed, Viola Monte was the glue that held the James organization together.

She was a smart, strong woman. In addition to her duties in the Harry James Orchestra office, she managed to raise her two children Hallei and Frank Jr.

She was the person who had to deal with Harry's personal life. She delivered checks and gifts to Harry's family, friends, and acquaintances. When Sonny Payne was dying in the Intensive Care Unit at Cedar Sinai Hospital, Viola delivered the check to pay for Sonny's medical bills and to help Sonny's family.

From 1969 until 1983, Viola would send me itineraries for the band's tours. Every year I got a Christmas card signed by Harry and an occasional birthday card.

All sent by Vi.

She would send me charts, or the odd piece of music that she thought I might like to have.

In 1982, I was touring across the country, playing in a Big Band out of Denver. I called Viola and told her when we would be in Los Angeles.

We were going to play a dance at Stevens Steakhouse in Commerce City, California. I commandeered the equipment van and drove to the Harry James Orchestra office.

Pee Wee and Viola met me at the door. They were both very warm and cordial. Pee Wee asked me if I had the trumpets that they had helped me get. I went to the van and carried my trumpet case inside.

Pee Wee said, "Let us hear you play it!"

I played a little of "Sleepy Lagoon" for them. Pee Wee saw my faded old Parduba mouthpiece, and said: "You can't play a beautiful horn like that, with that old mouthpiece!"

He reached in a desk drawer and pulled out a box of mouthpieces. He handed me a new gold-plated Parduba HJ 5* mouthpiece wrapped in tissue.

Viola invited me over to their house for lunch.

The Montes were gracious hosts. Vi insisted that I share their left-over Chinese food.

(I hate Chinese food!)

Pee Wee gave a tour of the house. Then we went out to the bar by the outdoor pool.

There was a half-gallon dispenser with a bottle of Smirnoff Vodka.

Pee Wee said, "That's Harry's when he comes over."

He explained that Harry would have been there, but he was attending the funeral for Harry Mills of the Mills Brothers, who had passed away on June 28, 1982.

We got into a discussion about the current state of the band. I played a tape for him that I had bought at a record store. It was a bootleg of the James band at the Monterey Jazz Festival in 1965.

He exploded.

"Where did you get that? That's a bootleg! I'm going to sue those bastards!"

He then called singer Ernie Andrews who was featured on the cassette tape.

The two of them complaining about the existence of the tape decided that somebody was going to pay!

That evening, Frank and Vi came to the Stevens Steakhouse to hear me perform. They sat at a table to the right of the stage.

Both of them were gracious and told me how much I sounded like Harry on "You Made Me Love You."

I talked to Viola a couple of times in 1983.

I didn't see her again until 2011.

In November of 2011, Cheryl and I went to Los Angeles to see Cheryl's son and daughter.

We were also going to be reunited with many of Cheryl's friends and fellow musicians. We had been invited to perform with Clyde Reisinger's Big Band in North Hollywood.

It was wonderful to hand out with Bob Rolfe, Art Depew, Pat Longo, and several other former members of the Harry James Orchestra.

Of course, our dear friend Viola Monte came to hear us.

She sat at the table with us and was as effervescent as ever. She was always optimistic about our music.

After the music was over, I walked her to her bright red Toyota. Her license plate was "MR TRPT 1."

She invited us to her house the next day.

I got to show her my new "Harry James Music Appreciation Group" on Facebook. She asked me to help her become a member.

Before we left Vi's house, she went to the garage and came back with several charts from the Harry James library.

She handed them to me and said, "Happy Birthday!"

It was my birthday.

In 2013, we returned to Los Angeles.

We went to visit Viola. We got to spend a couple of hours with her. She took us on a tour of the house, showing us her memories from her decades as the Harry James Orchestra secretary.

At one point, she handed me a mouthpiece box. It contained a Bach 7C Mt. Vernon mouthpiece.

She explained that Rafael Mendez had given it to Harry shortly before Mendez died, explaining that it was the mouthpiece that he had been playing the last few years of his musical career.

Viola's favorite recording was "Melancholy Rhapsody." She was thrilled when I played her a recording of me playing it.

She told me that she was so proud of me.

Once again, she gave me a few of Harry's arrangements.

She was always so giving to us. She truly appreciated Cheryl and I trying to keep Harry's legacy alive.

Viola continued to play tennis regularly until the last couple of years of her life. She loved to go to Maui every year.

On March 26, 2020, Viola passed away at her home. She had been sick for several months.

Viola Montalbano was 95 years old, and an inspiration to all of us who were privileged to know her.

Dick Maher

We can't be sure exactly when, and why Richard "Dick" Maher became a Harry James fan.

Sometime in the 1960s, Dick Maher began collecting, and eventually cataloging photos, newspaper and magazine clippings related to Harry James.

He started saving tapes of James' performances, in addition to his large record collection.

On the wall in Dick's "Harry James Room," was a certificate proclaiming Dick Maher to be the official "Band Historian" of the Harry James Orchestra.

It was signed by Harry himself.

I first heard about Dick Maher in the late 1970s. He was a major provider of radio broadcasts, and photos that graced the album covers of many Joyce Records of the James band.

He was also a major contributor to the International Harry James Appreciation Society in London, England.

Dick Maher was a part of my wife, Cheryl Morris's life, for over forty years. They became acquainted when Cheryl first sang with Harry James at the "Carnation Plaza" at Disneyland.

In 2011 and again in 2013, Cheryl and I were honored to spend afternoons in the "Harry James Room" at Dick and Pat Maher's home in Cerritos, California.

The Mahers were generous almost to a fault.

The last time we saw Dick Maher, he showed me his immense collection of everything, Harry James.

"The Harry James Room," was a shrine to Harry. Photos and record albums lined the walls.

There was a classic jukebox, which played nothing but Harry James' records.

The room was a refuge for Harry himself on many occasions.

There was a glass case, with the trumpet that appeared on the 1958 Capitol album "Harry's Choice."

There was a partially empty pack of Marlboros that was Harry's. One of the rare original Parduba mouthpieces was in the case, along with bottles of King valve oil.

Dick and Pat Maher were loving Friends.

I was honored to receive Dick's son Jim's memories of Harry James and his connection to his Dad:

"As I sit here writing this with the music of Harry James playing in the background, I am flooded with memories of my life. "Sleepy Lagoon," "It's Been A Long, Long Time," "You Made Me Love You," "I've Heard That Song Before," "Corner Pocket," to name just a few and, of course, "Melancholy Rhapsody," which was the last song my father heard before he passed and one I still have an equal amount of sadness and joy listening to."

"I was probably nine or ten when I first became aware of my father's passion for Harry James. It may have been because he wired every room in the house with speakers that, as I recall, only played Harry James. It may have been the weekend trips to hole in the wall record stores all around the Los Angeles area where together we would flip through stack upon stacks of records looking for anything that mentioned Harry James.

"It also may have been movie nights where my father would borrow a rather large projector from work and screen movies that happened to star, you guessed it, Harry James. I remember Springtime In The Rockies and Outlaw Queen, but I think he had them all. I have no idea how he acquired them since they were theatre grade, but he had them. It's also very likely that it could have been because every summer, my father would take his two weeks a year vacation and attend Harry's annual gig at Disneyland, which coincidentally was also two weeks a year!!!"

"Now, my father spent eight years in the military. Four years in the Navy and four years in the Air Force. During his naval years, he was a Photographers Mate, which led to his love for photography. He had a darkroom and several cameras one of which was a Speedgraphic camera, which for those that don't know, was a rather large camera that sat on a tripod with a little curtain in the rear that you put your head into so you could view the image that would be transferred to a

4x5 inch negative. Well, my father would take the Speedgraphic to Harry's gigs, and very quickly, he became noticed by Peewee Monte (Harry's manager) as well as Harry himself. My father would take the photos home and during the day (since he was on vacation) develop the film in his darkroom and print out 8x10 inch photos which he would take that night to the gig and have Harry sign."

"He would also take photos of the other band members and give them copies which led to friendships with some of the band most notably Corky Corcoran, who became very close with my father for many years. After a year or two of taking the Disneyland photos, Peewee made my father the official band photographer, which allowed us free admission to Disneyland entering through a special entrance as well as a bunch of free Disneyland ticket books for us kids. A couple of nights each summer, my parents allowed us to bring a friend, which made us very popular in the neighborhood. I have many memories of falling asleep as the night went on to the sounds of Harry James and his band."

"I recall two times Harry came to our house during the day before a gig and would have dinner and tour the Harry James Room. This was the only time in our lives, and I might add that we would have steak enter our house. The good silverware would come out, and us brothers would be on our very best behavior. I think Harry really enjoyed visiting. I mean, who else had a room with a small dance floor with " The Harry James Room" cut into the black and white checkered floor!! I do know Harry gifted my father some items for the Harry James Room, two of which was a trumpet Harry had won in a trumpet competition years before as well as a hi-fi stereo that had belonged to Harry and Betty Grable. Boy, if that stereo could have talked!! Both of these items, as well as one of Harry's horns to this day, still resides in the Harry James room. Did I mention the hat Harry wore in Outlaw Queen? Yep, he has that too!!"

"My father was very humble about his collection and never bragged about just how much he had. He didn't have to; what was important to him was the man and his music. One of my father's proudest moments was when Harry wanted to use one of his photos to be the band's publicity photo. Peewee asked how much for the rights, and my father said one buck. So he received a check from the band for one dollar, signed by Harry. My father, of course, framed it and it hangs prominently in the Harry James room to this day."

"Through the years, my father enjoyed a close personal relationship with Vi and Peewee. They were really good to my parents, and my father so appreciated that. After Peewee passed, my father got to know Peewee's brother Sal and also stayed in contact with Vi, who both my parents thought the world of. She was such an interesting and kind lady."

"After Harry passed, my father continued his passion with the band. Whenever we would visit or call, it was a sure bet my father was upstairs, transcribing Harry's music from his collection. He had his stopwatch where he would time each song along with notes about the recordings. We called it his never-ending project, and sure enough, he was still working on it up until the time he became ill. He had also discovered eBay by this time and acquired many additional mementos for his collection, but that's another story!"

By Jim Maher April 2020

Cheryl Morris-Vocalist

I was delighted to have been associated with The Harry James Orchestra for ten years, and only became a member of the band by somewhat of a fluke.

Eventually, I was informed that the vocalist they had hired had been struggling for quite some time with her voice. When my former husband, (husband-to-be at that time), trumpeter Clyde Reasinger, (who was also a member of the band at that time), heard Harry was looking for someone new who could do road tours and perform locally with the band, Clyde told Harry and manager Pee Wee Monte that I could easily fit in to help them out. That I knew a wide variety of standards and was already a busy and seasoned vocalist in Los Angeles for more than a few years.

Clyde said they seemed instantly intrigued but wanted to hear me sing, so Clyde gave them some tapes of me performing with Clyde's own big band, and I must have passed 'muster' as they immediately sent me three cassettes of Harry's charts, each one with various vocalists singing the tunes. Fortunately, I knew almost all the vocal arrangements already from a lifetime of listening to and loving Harry's great vocalists, such as Helen Forrest & Kitty Kallen.

As I recall, there were only about four or five charts unfamiliar to me on these cassettes, they had sent me, but I practiced all of them well and quickly 'nailed' each one down. Within no time, I was hired and went down to Harry's business office and signed papers. This was sometime in late January or early February of 1979.

I was now the new Harry James Orchestra vocalist, but, my first 'trial run gig' would not be until one night in March of 1979 at The Golden West Ballroom in Norwalk, California. This would become the gig that would stand out like no other in my memory for the rest of my life.

On that 1st night, I remember feeling quite relaxed and more than confident in my ability to get through the evening's program list of vocal tunes. But, whether Harry himself would seriously be interested in me remaining with the band afterward remained to be seen. After meeting Mr. James that night, I must admit, I was a bit frightened of him.

Even though I had never spoken to Harry James before, I had been around the band quite a bit through the years as I'd had several close friends who had played in Harry's band in years past. It was not uncommon for many of us to go, perhaps to Disneyland, wherever to hear our friends play with the HJ band.

Now, my fiancé, Clyde, had been on the band for many months, and so I had been attending gigs whenever possible with Clyde, just to listen with other girlfriends or wives of band members, but still had not met Harry, only viewing the man from afar. After much time observing Harry James, and knowing of his illustrious career as well as I did, he was, for me, of the superstar status. A sophisticated and legendary musical giant. I thought to myself, "I know I can get them through this gig, and perhaps a few more gigs temporarily, but surely he will want to hire someone more well known, more exciting, so I thought this first night would probably be my last" but, as strange as it seemed to me, as Harry would later put it, "just the very opposite happened!"

Meeting Mr. Harry James formally right before the concert dance was far from a 'warm and fuzzy' experience. It was somewhat terrifying to me, but I refused to let it show.

Harry was seated in his dressing room backstage at The Golden West Ballroom when Frank "Pee Wee" Monte's dear wife and band secretary, Viola Monte led me backstage to meet Him.

She said, "Harry, this is Cheryl Morris." He looked up at me and said in a bit of a snarl, "Do you know "But Not for Me?" And I said, enthusiastically, "YES!" Then he quickly snarled again, almost overlapping my comment and replied, "Yeah, but do you know OUR arrangement?" Before I could even answer, he said, "I play so many bars then it modulates to you, then you sing so many bars, and it modulates back down to me. Can you do it? And I again said, "YES!" Fine! After that, I was swiftly escorted out, and that was my first introduction to Mr. Harry James.

In a matter of minutes, I was standing in the wings holding a piece of yellow lined paper with all the songs I was to sing written on it for the four sets prepared for the evening, so stood there listening to the band wail, waiting to go out to sing my first song on the list, "Embraceable You."

Soon the big moment arrived. Harry briefly announced my name, and out I went. The piano gave me my intro for the tune, and after I'd finished singing it, Harry was now, miraculously, all smiles! That sour face had brightened up, and he quickly turned into seemingly 'another person!' The grump I'd just met moments ago was now officially gone! Suddenly it all became great fun, and I don't remember making one mistake all evening. The entire evening went more than well. Actually, 'like water off a rock.'

By the end of the evening, Harry's people, everyone was coming up to me telling me how happy Harry was, that he was 'raving' about me. That I had obviously 'hit the ball out of the park,' and that Mr. James was elated! To say I was in shock would be a complete understatement.

That was the beginning of my time working alongside Mr. Harry James. From that moment on, Harry was great to me and even included me in many performances his girl singers were not necessarily hired to be a part of, ever insisting to various promoters they take me. I was beyond grateful to him, and always will be for believing in me and being such an incredible friend to me, with no strings attached, if you know what I mean, for several years before he died.

I was so incredibly grateful to Harry and his wonderful managers that even after Harry had passed, in July of 1983, they asked me if I would stay and continue to sing with the band. I simply could not say no and so remained the only girl vocalist with The Joe Graves and Art Depew HJ Ghost band(s) for the next seven years.

The Sideman's Perspective- The Musicians who were there:

Over the last fifty years, I have learned so much from the Musicians, Vocalists, and Friends who were part of the Harry James musical Family.

When I started writing this book, I invited former members of the Harry James Orchestra to tell stories about how they joined the band. And interesting stories from their days with Harry James.

I began by asking them all to answer a questionnaire. The questions were simple, and all related to when they and how they became members of the Harry James Orchestra.

It was a heartwarming and great encouragement in the way that every one of the musicians I contacted willingly participated.

Harry James Alumni Questionnaire

Name-

Years active with the Harry James Orchestra-

Position in band-

How did you become a member of the James Orchestra-?

Please relate a story about Harry's skill and musicianship?

Please tell us about one gig that stands out for you-

Thank you so much for your contributions to my Harry James book- Chuck

This portion of the book will be the answers to those questions.

Alan Kaplan-

Alan Kaplan has long been one of the top studio trombone players in Los Angeles. His recording credits vary vastly from Marvin Gaye to Johnny Mathis to Madonna to Placido Domingo to Sarah Vaughan to Oingo Boingo to Whitney Houston to the Hollywood Bowl Orchestra, Josh Groban, Michael Buble, Paul McCartney, Bob Dylan, Lady Gaga, and countless more. He has played on the scores for nearly 1000 movies and thousands of television episodes.

Years active with the Harry James Orchestra- 1974 and 1975

Position in band-Lead Trombone

How did you become a member of the James Orchestra-?

While I was still working with Buddy Rich Pee Wee Monte called me. He said Harry was looking for a lead trombone player and offered me $350 a week. I asked if I could think it over since our schedule with Buddy was looking sparse, and the turnover in the band wasn't, in my mind, beneficial. That night Buddy gave the whole band two weeks' notice. He was laying off the band to open a club in New York and play with a trio. The next day I called Pee Wee and told him I'd like to take the job but needed $400 a week. Fortunately, he went for it, and I started with them only ten days after my gig with Buddy finished.

Please relate a story about Harry's skill and musicianship

When I was with the band, Harry usually played note-for-note the same jazz solos every night. We were also encouraged to do the same. I think that was kind of an old-school big band thing. Some night, though, Harry would be inspired and would call up some different charts and play some amazing solos. A lot of the old charts had him playing lead, and it was amazing. We had a rehearsal in L.A. one time, and he was trying to describe to our lead trumpet player how he wanted something phrased. Finally, Harry went back behind the trumpets and played the lead part himself. It was brilliant. He still had it back then, but he didn't choose to show it very often.

Please tell us about one gig that stands out for you-

One gig that was special for me was at the World's Fair in Spokane. We played a morning concert that day. When it came to Sleepy Lagoon, I, for some reason, decided to play the solo on the bridge in one breath. I could circular breathe but hadn't done that solo that way before. Harry was so impressed that he pointed it out to the audience and had me come down front and do it again. The next day he called the King Musical Instrument Company and told them I was going to be a superstar, and they should get me with them. The next day I spoke to King, and they sent me two trombones and made me an artist/clinician.

Thanks for reaching out, Chuck. Give my best to Cheryl!

Alan

Bill Hicks

Years active with the Harry James Orchestra- Feb. 1976 - Aug. 1979

Position in band- Split lead trumpet

When I joined, I took Sanford Skinner's place. The book was about evenly split 50/50. During the first few months Harry would occasionally turn around and tell us to switch parts when he thought that tune was better suited for the other player. As time went on Harry was getting frustrated with the lead player and started giving me more 1st parts. Harry wasn't happy with the next couple of guys that were hired on the lead book, and I ended up doing about 65% of the lead. During my last year, Clyde Reasinger was hired, Harry liked Clyde, so the books went back to a 50/50 split.

How did you become a member of the James Orchestra-?

Pee Wee asked Claude Gordon for a recommendation. I was hired to play a ballroom gig on a Saturday night. At the end of the night, Pee Wee said Harry says the job is yours if you want it. Then he told me to be at ABC studios the next Tuesday morning where we filmed the "John Denver and Friend" T.V. special with Frank Sinatra.

Please relate a story about Harry's skill and musicianship

I had been on the band a few months when we recorded "The King James Version." We recorded two 3-hour sessions a day for 5 days. I noticed Harry wasn't playing the same solos I had heard him play every night. He would play a new solo then on each subsequent take he would make some changes or throw out that solo and play something completely different. On the next job after the sessions, when we played one of the songs, we had recorded Harry is playing a new solo, not the same one I had heard every night before the recording sessions. He continues playing those same new solos every night. When the album comes out a few months later, I put it on the turntable, and those "new solos" are the ones that made it onto the record.

Harry was the most consistent player I ever heard. The only time I could hear something wasn't quite right was when Harry had spent the day in the dentist's chair getting his implants adjusted.

Chuck Par-Due in the late '70s, about the first 45 charts were in order for our typical 4-hour dance job. Start with number one and just keep turning over the next chart. Didn't deviate from that too often, and when he did, you usually knew what he was going to call like instead of #27, he would occasionally do #72. For a 2-hour concert, it would be 22-

24 tunes (out of that first 45) in a similar order. In my last two years on the band, I never looked at the book but always had it sitting on the music stand just in case.

Please tell us about one gig that stands out for you-

The gig that stands out the most is the John Denver TV special. Denver is telling how Frank started with Harry, Sinatra sings a couple of songs with us. Then he tells how Frank left to join Tommy Dorsey's band, and Frank walks across the stage and sings a few songs with the Dorsey band. After that, he talks about all the great Capitol albums made with Nelson Riddle. Franks goes to center stage where Nelson has a large orchestra, and they do several of the big hits. Then John talks about how Sinatra worked in Vegas with the Count Basie band and the albums the made. The three combined bands start playing "April In Paris" while Basie walks on stage and sits down at the piano. The three bands accompany Sinatra and Basie on 5 or 6 of their big hits then ended with "My Way."

Dave Stone

My name is Dave Stone. I'm a bass player. I was with the Harry James Orchestra in the last few days of 1975 and most of 1976. My dad, Bob Stone, also a bass player, played with Harry from 1949-1951. He played a cruise and a few gigs with Harry in 1975 and kind of held the gig for me until I got off the road with Stan Kenton. I was playing with Woody and Stan in1975, and when my dad mentioned that to Pee Wee, that was enough to convince them to hire me. After I got off the road with Kenton, I had one day off and started the next day with Harry.

I was amazed at how Harry played great every gig. He was always nice to the band members. It was awesome to get to work with Harry, a true legend.

We were on one of the 6-week tours that year, and we're playing a concert. Sonny Payne was on the drums, and of course, he was awesome. During his drum solos, he was well known for hitting his drumsticks, and when they bounced off, he would catch them in midair. But in this one concert, the stick flew out of control right by me, and I caught that stick. It was a funny, wild moment that I'll never forget.

Bill Barrett

Years active with the Harry James Orchestra- 1979-1983

Position in band-

How did you become a member of the James Orchestra-?

Bill Hicks was leaving the band and asked if I was interested, so Clyde Reasinger arranged for Pee Wee Monte to hear me play on some lead in Clyde's band at local 47, and that's how I got in the band.

Please relate a story about Harry's skill and musicianship

Harry knew everyone's part, so you always had to be on your toes! One particular gig, the 2nd tenor sax (Norm Smith), left the stand to go to the bathroom, and on the next tune, Norm had a duet with the first tenor (Ed Easton). Harry simply walked and stood next to Ed; and played Norm's part!

Please tell us about one gig that stands out for you-

We were playing in a theater in the round in upstate New York, and as the stage was rotating it made Harry nauseous, so he asked Les DeMerle (not sure of his last name's spelling) to sit out the set... and Harry proceeded to play drums the rest of the set! So many stories but not all related to his musical prowess... I appreciated the time I had playing with a living legend!

I would like to add that we were doing the "Big Broadcast Of 1944" at the Pantages Theater. In the middle of our month run, I was given my notice so I went to see Harry ask him why I was being let go so that in the future I could correct the problem he had with my playing... he said, "Well Babe, there's right field and left field, were in right field, and you're in left field"... whatever it meant to Harry, Pee Wee came to me that night and told me that I was back on the band.. but... of I started to play like I had before he'd have to fire me again... I never knew what it was but they did fire Larry Veo the lead player at the time of that show!

So many stories but thought you'd find it interesting...

Say "Hi" to Cheryl for me please, I enjoyed her singing as I thought she has a beautiful clear voice, and her style was perfect!

Hal Espinosa

I was on and off the band, I believe, between 1971 and when he died.

Mostly the lead chair.

I first worked with Harry when Pee Wee was in a panic for a trumpet player. Harry had a two-week job at Harrahs Hotel in Reno, and he needed a trumpet player. I was playing lead with Les Brown at the time, and it was a very slow period for Les, no T.V. Shows, and only two dance jobs. I explained to Les that Harry was the reason I took up the trumpet and what a thrill it would be for me to play on his band for the two weeks. Les let me take off, after first making sure I was coming back. After that, I traveled with Harry when he was in between lead players and when my schedule allowed. Harry wanted me to join the band full time, but I was doing too many TV Shows and record dates, along with a lot of Broadway Shows. So, I worked with him when I could. My last job with him was when we worked at the Century Plaza Hotel, and that was his last job before he died. He sounded the best he had in the last few years due mainly to his health issues. Best, I had heard him in years. I don't remember him even cracking a note, and yes, he used his vaseline more than anyone I know. He was a beautiful person and a beautiful and fantastic trumpet player.

To me, when I first heard him play in the late '40s, Harry was the best trumpet player I had ever heard, and I wanted to play the trumpet because of him. Once, when I worked on the band and got to know Harry, I told him that story why I took up the trumpet and ended it by telling him that most trumpet players around the time I was growing up, took up the trumpet because of him. I think he really liked hearing that because he got a big smile on his face. It wasn't until I went with the band to Buenos Aires, Argentina, to play three or four nights of "concerts" at the Opera House that I got to hear the old Harry James. He told me he practiced for this trip because we played some of the old flag-wavers that he normally didn't play during his regular dance sets. Harry was on top of his game in Buenos Aires and didn't miss a note. He showed us all what a great player he really was. His musicianship was there in his phrasing, his dynamics, his artistry and his sound. You hear him play, and you instinctively know it's Harry; he was one of a kind!

The one gig that stands out for me was his last gig at Century Plaza Hotel in Los Angeles. As you know, Harry was very sick; he missed a job in Bakersfield, where Ray Anthony showed up in his place because Harry was in the hospital for treatment. A short time later, we were playing that job at the Century Plaza with Harry out in front of the band. We were playing to a large crowd, so the ballroom was opened up to its full capacity. Because of that the Hotel had a camera recording the band and it was being used to project the image of the band to the crowd on either end of the ballroom. At that time, I was a Trustee on the Local 47's Executive Board, and Pee Wee knew it, so he made sure that the recording was destroyed after the job ended. It was very unfortunate because Harry played great, sounded better than ever, didn't crack a note, and seemed to have gotten his life back. He sounded like his old self, but a few days later, maybe a week or two, I was awakened by a phone call from a local radio station informing me that Harry had died and wanted an interview. I was shocked! He was my idol since I was a kid, and now, he was dead.

Sorry Chuck, writing this brought back some happy and unhappy memories. It was a great loss to me and many, many others, you included.

I hope this works for you. If not, let me know.

My best to you and Cheryl. ... Hal

Marty Harrell

Years active with the Harry James Orchestra- Approximately 1966-67

Position in band- Bass Trombone

How did you become a member of the James Orchestra-?

I took Dave Wheeler's place

Please relate a story about Harry's skill and musicianship

Harry had a sound like nobody else. He sang through the horn. His projection was incredible.

Please tell us about one gig that stands out for you-

We had just finished the gig and were on the bus ready to leave, and I hear this voice saying, "Marty, Come up here" It was Harry. I thought, "what did I do wrong now? I go up, and Harry said, "Have a seat" He then handed me a glass of vodka and said, "I assume you like this stuff?" I said "YEP" He then continued to compliment my playing. Then he said "get your bell out of the stand and let all the people that paid to hear you know what you sound like" I then started to return to my seat, and he said "one more thing if you're gonna drink that stuff, EAT WELL! That was my music lesson with the GREAT Harry James!

Good Luck with your book!

Mike Butera

Years active with the Harry James Orchestra- 1977-79

Position in band-solo Tenor Sax

How did you become a member of the James Orchestra-? I was appearing as a soloist with a big band that was opening for the group "SuperSax" in Sacramento. One of the members, Lanny Morgan, heard me play and we exchanged numbers as I was going to be recording in L.A. the next week and we were going to get together. Harry asked Lanny to take the featured saxophone position that Corky Corcoran had held for 35 years. Corky had come down with cancer. But he was not available to go on tour and instead, he recommended me for the chair. Harry's manager, "Pee Wee," called me, and I flew down to L.A. for a weird audition! We met at someone's house, and just the saxophone section and pee wee were there. We played through some of the charts, and then the section played long tones to provide chords for 12 bar blues for me to solo over.

That was it! The first gig was at a mall in L.A. and the great Basie band singer, Joe Williams showed up and asked Harry if he could sit in. So my first gig was with Joe Williams singing.

Please relate a story about Harry's skill and musicianship

Harry was a true master on the trumpet. Flawless technique and great articulation. And his range was so impressive. The world has never seen a better trumpet player. Miles always said that the trumpet player he looked up to the most was Harry.

Please tell us about one gig that stands out for you-

In 1977 we played at the Newport jazz festival for the "big band day." Every major big band was playing that day; Cat Anderson led a "house band" from New York City. The bands that I remember being there were Count Basie, Duke Ellington (w/ Mercer leading as the Duke has just passed), Thad Jones and Mel Lewis Jazz Orchestra, Toshiko Akioshi and Lew Tabakin Big Band, Buddy Rich Orchestra, Stan Kenton Orchestra (Stan was at the end. I sat next to him backstage as his band was preparing to go on and he was very sick) and Maynard Ferguson's band, plus a surprise special guest band. That was the Harry James Orchestra!

Well, we had the exciting opportunity to meet and visit with all the legends of the big band era in the huge dressing room area that all the bands hung out in. I'll never forget the friendly visit with Pepper Adams, who jumped into our tour bus to greet us when we arrived, the great Al Grey, Lock-Jaw Davis, Frank Foster, Thad Jones, and many others. What a privilege!

But what happened when we went on, I'll NEVER FORGET. The Buddy Rich Big Band just finished their set, Buddy's band were quickly tearing down as the house band played. We got set up. The curtains open. The huge audience applause and hoots rang out as the "Surprise Big Band" was Harry James! After the opener that only lasted 30 seconds, we immediately begin an uptempo tune called "Apples" that featured the great Sonny Payne on a long drum solo. Now Sonny, having been Basie's drummer and Frank Sinatra's favorite drummer, was a legend. And of course before Buddy Rich went out on his own, he had been Harry's featured drummer and the highest-paid sideman at the time. Sonny and Buddy did not like each other. They had an major ego conflict for years. Stories would get out on the big-band gossip circuit about buddy saying harsh things about Sonny and vice versa. They hated each other even though if they met publicly, they would be friendly. Well, as Harry kicked off the tune, something felt wrong. That loud snare drum of Sonny's was not accenting the percussive phrases of the arrangement. (Sonny was the loudest drummer I have ever played with!) I looked up a Harry, and he was glaring at Sonny. After several measures, the band whimpered to a halt like a car out of gas. Sonny stood up on his drum stand and held up his snare drum to show the audience that his drum head had been having been slit with a knife!

Well, I hear applause start up again, and here comes Buddy with a smile on his face, carrying his snare drum to hand it to Sonny to play!

We all felt Sonny's pain as we finished that set that day. And on the tour bus for the next few weeks, we listened to Sonny's lament: "that damn Buddy, I know he did it."

Rita Graham-Vocalist

I was active with the Harry James Orchestra from 1971 to 1973.

I became a member of the James Orchestra because my friend, singer Janice Harrington introduced me to the Harry James drummer, Sonny Payne. In 1969 I'd recorded the album, "Rita Graham Vibrations," produced by Ray Charles for Ray's Tangerine Label. "Vibrations," except for one track that is a Northern Soul hit, is a collection of lush American Songbook Standards. It is the only major project Ray Charles produced for a female artist on his label. I was amazed that Sonny offered to take the album to Harry James, and even more amazed and overjoyed a few days later, when band manager, Peewee Monty called and offered me the gig.

With only a few days to meet the band at Las Vegas' Desert Inn Casino, arranger Charles Blaker stayed up all night to write three charts that I placed on the conductor's podium, with shaking hands.

Mr. James nodded to me, glanced at my charts, and asked, "What's this?" In a small voice, I answered, "My charts, Sir." He shuffled through the pages, then after a long silence, he counted off, "1-2-3!"

The band kicked in "Charade" that can be viewed on the "Harry James/Rita Graham in London" Video Post on YouTube.

Working with The Harry James Orchestra was one of the greatest experiences of my life. During every performance, I was thrilled to stand backstage and hear Harry's beautiful, haunting solos of the wonderful music that will forever play in my heart. It was a revelation to feel the audience's enthusiasm for every moment of every concert, as the crowds gathered close around the bandstand.

One of my favorite Gigs was New Orleans, Mardi Gras, when we played the Bacchus Ball with Phil Harris at the Rivergate Convention Center. Phil Harris was the Bacchus King. The parade ended there at the Rivergate, and it was awesome to see the entire parade, led by the Southern University Marching Band playing the theme from "Shaft," park all the floats around the room.

The Harry James Orchestra was especially 'Hot' that night!

Harry had an entire audience mesmerized during a concert when he played, "I Cover The Waterfront," accompanied only by pianist Jack Perciful. There was something about that moment that brought tears to my eyes. I realized that it wasn't just me~ most of the crowd, and the band members were moved.

I went to hear the band when they toured with "The Big Broadcast of 1944" Show with Gordon MacCrae. Harry and the band sounded great. I hung out backstage with him, hugged him, and took the opportunity to let him know how much he, the band, and his music had enriched my life.

Tommy Porrello

Years active with the Harry James Orchestra- 1964-- 1969

Position in band- Lead Trumpet

How did you become a member of the James Orchestra-?

Harry called Stan Kenton, the band I played lead for in 1963 and asked who played lead for him, as Stan was not going out in 64 & Harry's people called me. I was living in New York City at that time.

Please relate a story about Harry's skill and musicianship

Harry had some dental implants put in. We were off for about a month. I talked with Harry, and he said he might have to switch to a cornet and play like Bobby Hackett.

The first night on the road, we didn't know what to expect. Well, he played the shit out of everything. He sounded as good or better than ever.

Please tell us about one gig that stands out for you-

The night we played at the Monterey Jazz Festival. I walked in with Harry and coming to greet Harry was Miles Davis, others like Dizzy, Clark Terry, and some others I don't remember. He was admired by all of them; in fact, they came out on the stage and played on a Blues thing with Harry. Believe it or not, they also sang some.

Thank you very much,

Tommy!

Tony Scodwell

Position in the band: Hired on first trumpet 1963, section trumpet through 1966, first trumpet 1968-69.

How I became a member of the H.J. Orchestra: Recommended by Stan Kenton

The trumpets would do a little choreography on this and other things we'd play all the time. I'm not sure how those things got started, but most road bands tended to get into routines over a period of time.

When I first joined Harry in 1964, Nick Buono hipped me to things that were unwritten and had become part of what Harry expected to see and hear. For instance, you had better get the soli down pat in "The Mole" because Harry would be listening to you waiting to come on. Also, Nick said to learn Harry's part on the theme [Ciribiribin] as there would be a night somewhere where you'd be playing it.

Harry never got sick, but the time he had his bottom teeth implanted Stan Kenton fronted the band and I played the opening theme. That was kind of cool for me as Stan had recommended me for the gig while I was on his band that was breaking up after the tour in England was over a few months earlier. Harry always said he wasn't running a farm team; he expected guys to come on the band ready to play.

The first few nights up in Tahoe, I didn't have a clue as to what tunes Harry was calling. Nick said to memorize the first 20 tunes most frequently called, and I'd be fine. Yeah, right! Harry would turn around after the cutoff and shout..." Shiny, choo, chree fo" in rhythm, which of course meant, "Shiny, two three four and was his immediate count off for "Shiny Stockings'. It took about a month, and I wasn't opening the book up at all. I am so glad to have been there.

Harry's skill and musicianship: Photographic memory and kicked tunes off at perfect tempo. Fantastic stamina and incredible agility on the trumpet. His sound was warm and fat.

Favorite gig(s): The Monterey Jazz Festival in 1965 and Carnegie Hall concert (first since H.J. was with Benny Goodman.

I hope this is OK for your needs. Anything I can do to help, just let me know.

I hope this adds to your collection and let's keep spreading the word.

All the best!

Tony

Fred Radke

Position: lead trumpet

Years: 1969-1970

1972 2weeks

1974 1 week(closing Worlds Fair, Spokane)

How I became a member;

I was recommended to Harry

By Joe Venuti and Corky Corcoran

Most rememberable gig:

There were so many, but the one that I remember most was my last two weeks on the band we recorded at RCA in Hollywood for Reader Digest where we did at six set LP series of Harry James and Helen Forrest

Harry was superb.

I used to witness Harry walking out on the stand and playing things that guys in the band would just look at each other and say how does he do that. To me, all performances were a memorable experience

No one will ever play like Harry James. He was the best.

PS

I want to thank you for all of your research and time you spend on the history of Harry, like the book Trumpet Blues it didn't focus on his musicality and his contribution to big band jazz and trumpet playing.

As Sal Monte said, keep the flame alive and what I'm doing leading the band and your appreciation group and performing his music.

Sometimes we should talk I have many stories

All the Best to you and your family.

Regards,

Fred

Michael Millar

Years active with the Harry James Orchestra- May 1980 (Big Broadcast in S.F.) to June 1983 (last gig at Century Plaza) with Harry; ghost band with Joe Graves and Art DePew, 1985-2003(?) with some gaps when they toured, and I didn't go.

Position in band- Bass trombonist

How did you become a member of the James Orchestra-? Heard Rich Bullock was leaving, recommended by Steve Tyler.

Please relate a story about Harry's skill and musicianship- For future consideration

Tony Crapis

I spent two years as Lead Trumpet from 1981-83.

I was recommended by Tommy Porrello. I auditioned at Carnation Plaza at Disneyland in August of 1981.

Harry could play a gig after an eight-hour bus ride, warm up right on the spot, and sound great.

On his Jazz solos, he always played the right notes. He was very musical, and that sound. You knew it was Harry James!

In April of 1982, we played a week's gig at the Fairmont Hotel in San Francisco. It was a beautiful theater; the sound was incredible. You could hear every note.

Harry sounded great as usual.

Another time, we played in Davenport, Iowa. I went to an old-style diner/coffee house for breakfast.

Harry was sitting at the counter, so I sat next to him.

The waitress asked, "What are you boys in town for?"

I told her that we are playing a concert that night.

She asked what group we were playing with.

I said, "Harry James."

The waitress replied, "Oh Harry James died years ago."

(Maybe she got confused, Betty Grable maybe.)

Harry laughed and pulled out his driver's license. He handed it to her.

We all laughed, and he invited her to the concert that night!

About the author

In a musical career that has spanned almost fifty years, Chuck Par-Due has toured the country as a trumpet soloist and vocalist with several prominent big bands and jazz combos. In 1986, Chuck had the privilege of performing for President Ronald Reagan. That same year, Chuck had the honor of performing for soon to be President George H. Bush. In 1999, Chuck performed for the NEC World Series of Golf, and witnessed a Tiger Woods victory.

In addition, Chuck Par-Due has been featured on numerous radio and television shows and has appeared at some of the most prestigious venues all the way from California to Florida. As a trumpet player, Chuck has performed the music Of Harry James, Glenn Miller and other big band giants. Chuck has performed with some of the most famous musicians and bands of all time, including: Bob Haggart, Helen Forrest, the Jimmy Farr Orchestra, the Pete Wagner Orchestra, the Queen City Jazz Band, Lee Arrellano, Joni Janek, and many others.

Chuck met Harry James in 1970 as a sixteen-year-old. They remained friends until Harry's death in 1983.

Contact information- email-*chuckparduebigband@yahoo.com*

Join the Harry James Music Appreciation Group on Facebook

https://www.facebook.com/groups/Harryjamesgroup

Printed in Great Britain
by Amazon